FOR
STORMBOY

FOR STORMBOY

CRAIG ROBINSON

atmosphere press

To those who said
I couldn't, wouldn't, or shouldn't, I did it!

PROLOGUE

Anton kept his duffle bag tight on his shoulder, making his way through the streets of Westside. It was early in the evening, and he knew how important this drop was to his employer. He was never allowed to look inside the bags or ask about the nature of the deal, but it paid well, and that's all that really mattered. Tony had really helped him out with this job. Times were hard for Anton after losing his mother in a gang shooting over in the market district. It had been hard for him to make ends meet. Being just out of high school and having no family to fall back on, this was the best he had.

The streets were alive, as usual. The sound of music playing throughout the night sky, animating the cold concrete buildings. Westside was always a boring town to him. It was the amateur musicians littering the streets every night with their symphonies that kept it interesting. He should be out there with them, but this damn job!

"Anton?"

A voice took him by surprise. So focused on staying hidden, he hadn't expected to hear his name. A familiar voice called to him. "Anton, over here!"

"Hey Nikki," Anton replied. Of all times to run into her. Her thick-rimmed glasses and innocent smile found him even in this large crowd.

"I was about to set up. Did you want to come and play a set with me?"

It was then that Anton noticed her violin case. She was just like him. A victim of circumstance. She had been accepted to a prestigious music academy, but who here in Westside could afford that? She was doomed like him to walk these streets, getting by despite all her talents.

"I really can't. I have something else I have to get to right now."

"I was hoping we could do this song I wrote together. Look." She took out a folder filled with sheet music, and handed it to him.

"I'm sorry Nikki—next time. I'm not prepared." He inched further and further from her. At this rate he was going to be late for the drop.

"Is your guitar not in the bag?" she said, moving toward him. Anton jumped back.

"No!" he exclaimed. "This is nothing."

Shocked, she reeled back.

"Sorry." Nikki placed her hand on her chest. "Well, will you at least look at the song? I think it would be good for us to get together. Like old times."

Anton could barely hear her through the commotion on the street.

"I'm sorry Nikki. I have to go right now!" Anton rushed away from her. He didn't look back, but he could still feel her disappointed gaze drilling into the back of his neck. He would have to make this up to her somehow, someday. But for now, this was too important.

The street life of downtown Westside gave way to Anton's true destination—the older downtown area before the city expanded northward, moving all the newer and more popular places to the updated, more modern part of town. They had aptly nicknamed it "Oldtown." It was always darker here, somehow, even when the sun was shining on it. The old rundown grey cement buildings created a canopy which blocked the sun, casting the streets in shadows for most of the day. Anton avoided this part of town if possible. Who could he be meeting in a place like this? Anton hiked the strap of the duffel bag higher on his shoulder and pressed on. Unlike the hustle and bustle of downtown, Oldtown was filled with shady street dwellers. Their eyes followed Anton as he made his way through the streets. But something else felt off. Like he was being watched from somewhere he couldn't quite see. He took a second to look around, but he couldn't spot anything out of the ordinary. At least not out of the ordinary for Oldtown.

"Let's get this over with," he thought.

Anton reached the drop point, a large run-down apartment building towering ten stories high. He pressed the button on the door labeled "6B" and waited. His mind wandered to Nikki and the sheet music she gave him. He took a few seconds while he was waiting to look it over. It was beautiful. He hummed the melody to himself, imagining what flourishes and personal touches he could add. It was just his style. He mimed how his fingers would glide up and down the neck of the guitar. Did she write this specifically for him?

"What do you want?" The voice on the intercom startled him.

"Tony sent me," he replied nervously. Silence followed for a moment.

"Wait right there." Anton's hand went directly to the bag to make sure it was still intact, just in case. That strange feeling crept up on him again.

"I hate Oldtown."

The door to the building opened, and a man slipped out. His eyes were dull and sunken, as if he hadn't slept in days. He analyzed Anton carefully up and down.

"Is that the stuff?" he asked.

"Yeah, here." Anton might have time to make it back to Nikki at this rate. He proceeded to take the bag off his shoulder.

"Naw!" the man exclaimed. "You're coming with me."

"But the job was to deliver the bag here to you."

5

"Well, now the job is to come with me to the meet." The man seemed insistent, but Anton really wanted to head back with Nikki. The thought of playing that piece she wrote took over his mind.

"Come on man, Tony said that wasn't the deal!" Anton tried to hand him the bag.

"Well, I'm changing the deal!" The man pulled out a gun from behind him and pointed it right into Anton's face.

"OK. OK." One hand fell on the bag and the other, with Nikki's folder in it, went straight in the air in a defensive posture. None of his jobs had been like this before. Get the package, go to the necessary spot, and drop it off. Done and done. If he was on time, the job was the easiest thing in the world! What had Tony gotten him into? The man ushered Anton down the steps of the stoop and down the street.

"And what the hell is this?" The man ripped the folder out of his hands.

"Hey, leave that alone."

"Shut up!" The man flipped through the pages before chucking the folder behind him.

"Please—those are important to me."

"More important than your life?" He pushed the tip of the gun into Anton's back, forcing him along. "Move!"

The pages of sheet music scattered and blew down the street behind them as Anton forced himself forward. "I'm sorry, Nikki."

The two of them wandered the streets of Westside, a gun placed firmly against Anton's back. He started humming to himself—the music she had made specifically for him. Despite having a gun to his back, it relaxed him.

"Shut up! We're here." They were at an intersection in a particularly barren part of Oldtown. Anton couldn't remember the last time he had been this far south. The man ushered him inside an abandoned multiplex with its broken neon lights and busted-out windows. Upon entering, the sound of broken glass under their feet echoed through the empty halls of the theater.

"Don't take another step," a voice from within called to them. Anton froze, and the man hid behind him. "You were supposed to come alone."

"Well, things change. The kid here is a third party. Make sure nothing stupid happens here." The man had said this while cowering behind him. Anton began to sweat, his eyes darting back and forth, trying to discern where the other voice could be coming from. The room was large! A desk near the door separated the rest of the hall, which broke into 2 large corridors at the back of the building. Between those, however, there was a derelict concession stand. That had to be it. There was nowhere else.

"Step inside so we can discuss how we are going to do this."

"No, you show yourself first!" A silence lingered in the hall as Anton wondered how he allowed himself to get into such a predicament. What kind of people was Tony wrapped up with? What was in those bags he had delivered before? After a long enough silence, a man stood up from behind the concession stand, gun pointed directly at Anton.

"You weren't followed I assume? They say Stormboy is out tonight!" The newly revealed man muttered into the echoed hall. He had on a backwards facing cap and a grimace that had smooshed his face together so hard it looked like it hurt.

"Naw, of course not." Anton couldn't help but remember that sneaking feeling he had earlier, but didn't dare to mention it now with guns pointed on either side of him. He never would've thought to look for Stormboy, honestly. Those electric powers of his seem to do more harm than good most of the time. People around here had strong opinions about their vigilante. Most hated him, calling him a dangerous menace. Others know what Westside is actually like and are happy he can show up to protect people. The man before him, Freight Train, was way more appreciated. His super strength was less threatening to the average person than millions of volts of electricity, Anton guessed. But why would the so-called defender of Westside follow him all the way out here? This was Westside; surely, he'd have more important things to do than to follow a stupid kid with a duffel bag to Oldtown. Unless. What was Anton carrying? The capped man put what looked like a grocery bag on the concession counter.

"The kid will drop the bag and get the stuff, and we'll all leave happy men." The man from behind Anton nudged him forward before giving a slight head nod toward the grocery bag. He started toward the bag.

"Slowly!" The capped man yelled. His gravelly voice, along with the echo in the hall, chilled Anton to his core. He began to walk as slowly as he could, while retaining a semblance of urgency. He was too terrified to glance anywhere other than the bag, which he made his destination. Anton began humming Nikki's song to himself, inching closer and closer until he finally reached the counter.

"Slowly take the bag and leave the other." Anton followed the instructions of the capped man, taking the new bag and returning to his old captor.

"You're almost there, Anton," Anton thought to himself, continuing to hum. He made it halfway back to the door before ...

"Don't move!" The deep, earthy voice of the capped man echoed once again through the hall, and Anton froze in place. "The bag is three Gs short!"

The sound of a gun cocking behind Anton made his heart stop. In an instant, he noticed the man standing by the entrance who led him here dive behind the desk near the entrance and a strange new voice he never heard before scream, "Everybody down!"

Anton followed his instruction instantly, tossing the bag to the side and diving to the ground with his hands over his head. He closed his eyes and made himself as small as possible. The sound of bullets filled the room. Anton began humming again, anything to keep out the carnage that was clearly going on around him. Another sound joined the barrage of bullets, however. It sounded to Anton like a downed powerline sputtering out of control. Flashes of lights shone behind his eyelids, but he refused to open them. It could have only been a moment, but to Anton it had felt like an eternity before all the violence around him settled.

"Hey, kid." That new voice.

Anton slowly opened his eyes. Hovering over him was a man, his eyes guarded by a mask making his eyes seem as white as milk and a black shirt with three spray-painted lightning bolts crudely drawn, stemming from his neck down the center and to either side of his torso.

"Stormboy," Anton whispered. The masked man offered a hand to help him to his feet. Anton looked toward the concession stand; the capped man must've been downed behind the counter, as he wasn't anywhere in sight. And his other "friend" shared a similar fate. He laid back against the front desk of the theater, gun just out of reach.

"Come on. Let's get you out of here," Stormboy said. How old was he? Anton always imagined him to be some old man, wise and experienced, but instead he couldn't be much older than him. The two walked out to the front, only stopping briefly for Stormboy to pick up the gun the man Anton was with was carrying. He took out the clip and all the bullets individually before chucking them in opposite directions into the darkness. As the two made it to the edge of the street, Anton finally saw him. He was a scrawny little thing barely an inch taller than him. The dangerous defender of Westside, the menace to society, as the news had led him to be, was no more than a kid like him.

"You going to be OK?" Stormboy continued.

Anton looked at him quizzically; nothing about this man was the man he had heard about.

"Yeah, I think so," Anton replied, still clearly shaken.

"So did Tony tell you he has you being a drug mule?" Stormboy's words cut, but after today's events, it really wasn't all that surprising. "You seem smarter than that, kid."

Stormboy reached behind him, in his back pocket, and pulled out a folder and handed it to Anton. Nikki's song!

"I'm pretty sure you have more important things to focus on." As Anton reached to grab the folder, tears began to well up in his eyes. The reality of his situation finally hit him.

"What am I supposed to do, then? You know what it's like in Westside. Tony gave me a way out, a job that could sustain myself. What are you going to give me, Stormboy?"

The hero of Westside paused for a moment and pondered.

"Honestly, I can't give you anything. But I can tell you, I'm not always going to be there for you like I was tonight. And I'm pretty sure that girl isn't going to want to see you laid out on the street, either."

Anton's eyes adjusted to his folder. Nikki, the only one who could truly relate to him. All she wanted to do was play with him, and he had almost gotten himself killed.

"So, you were following me?" Anton asked.

"From the moment you picked up the bag. Trust me, you don't want to be involved with Tony."

"Once he doesn't get his money, he will come for me."

"You tell him the truth," Stormboy said, which confused Anton at first. If he tells him Stormboy showed up, how could he be expected to complete the deal? "Pretty sure Nikki is waiting for you."

Stormboy turned to flee the scene, a tiny streak of electricity following in his motions across the street and up the fire escape. Anton couldn't understand; he had to know. He followed him across the street and shouted up to the rooftops to which he fled.

"Why do you do this? What's the point? I'm going to go home and still struggle to get by. And you! They will still hate you! So, what's the point! Why save me?"

Stormboy made it to the top of the building and paused. For a moment he looked back at Anton. Even behind his mask he could feel their eyes locked. However, without a word Stormboy fled into the night, leaving Anton in the cold silence of Oldtown. With nothing else, Anton made his way back to Downtown. The nightlife had really begun to kick off, and people were littering the streets. Anton's mind drifted. What was he supposed to do now? He couldn't work for Tony anymore, unless he wanted to get killed. But what else was there? Anton maneuvered through the crowd, only stopping when he heard the familiar sound of a violin that cut through all the noise of the streets and his mind alike. Anton looked up to see Nikki and all her poise. Her body majestically moved back and forth in time with her bow strokes. Her eyes gently closed behind her large round glasses. Anton began humming along to her performance. It was their song. She played as beautifully as she could, but something was missing. It was him. This song was meant for two. It was missing him! She was playing her heart out, but it wouldn't be perfect without the guitar portion of the piece, Anton's portion. The song played out in his head until her last note. The audience was clearly captivated. Why wouldn't they be? Nikki was master class, but Anton couldn't help but envision what it could've been. He joined in the ovation; she bowed in response with a bit of remorse on her face. Anton stooped toward the back of the crowd, avoiding her notice.

CHAPTER 1

ENTER STORMBOY

Sam leapt across from rooftop to rooftop, making his way toward the town center, the district in Westside where they kept City Hall and other important buildings which helped run the city. He managed to save the kid from Tony's plans tonight, but his night was far from over. Sam had really wished people would stop calling him Stormboy. It wasn't a name he particularly liked. His mentor, a hero named Freight Train, gave it to him. It was a sidekick's name, and he wasn't anyone's sidekick anymore. The fight with the two thugs in Oldtown wasn't as rough as he thought it would be, but he hadn't come out of it completely unscathed. One of the shots managed to clip him in his arm. Blood trickled down to his hand from underneath his sleeve.

Comes with the territory.

Being a hero meant throwing yourself into the line of fire like this. Just another day on the job. He rolled up his sleeve to inspect the damage. Nothing serious. He stretched his arm in a full circle to gauge mobility.

So, I won't lift my right arm above my head for the rest of the night. No big deal.

He wiped the blood with the hem of his shirt and proceeded with his patrol. He and his mentor had set pre-established routes that they would take every day, which covered the whole city. Eight in total that he switched up randomly over the nights of the week. It was important that no one could catch on to where and when he would be in any given place. "Be unpredictable; your enemy is always watching." One of the many mantras the great Freight Train had for him. He had so many mantras. They circled his head every day, the most prominent lesson being "Everything for them." Words he lived by. Freight Train had dedicated his life to this city, and he passed that responsibility on to him. It was duty that kept him out here every night—a promise he had to keep. But he couldn't help but remember that kid's words.

I saved him because it was the right thing to do. This is what you do. "*Everything for them!*"

An explosion went off a few blocks down. Looks like someone was trying to rob the Westside bank again.

Back to it.

Sam leapt into action. His night wasn't over quite yet. He navigated Westside as only he could. Leaping from rooftops and scaling fire escapes and hopping fences, the streets felt like home to him. No one knew them like he did. Well, maybe Freight Train did.

He soon arrived at the Bank. Still no police in sight. No offense, the fine officers of Westside—Sam was sure there were several crimes between here and there worth stopping. One thing that kid got right earlier, Westside was not an easy place to live. Freight Train did his best to clean this place up and now he was here to carry on that work. The bank alarms were blaring, but thankfully no one was around. Westside citizens kept to themselves in situations like this. It was safer that way. Made Sam's job easier, too.

Sam entered the building, stealthily taking in his surroundings. This wasn't his first time stopping a heist at this bank. It was the largest bank in Westside, so obviously it was a prime target for organized assaults like this. After all these years and all the money this place made, you think they would get better security. But with "Stormboy" here, they probably didn't incur as many losses as some other banks in equally rough cities.

I should start asking for a paycheck.

Upon looking at his surroundings, it looked as if there were four hostages tied up, mouths bound, one of which had a gunman gripping her hair, arguing. The bank had some waist-high floral décor that he was able to hide behind. He decided to let this play out a little.

"Turn off the damn alarm!" the gunman screamed. He had an assault rifle strapped to his back and a handgun placed firmly onto her chin. The girl was loudly crying. In between breaths, she tried to let out some words, but neither Sam nor the gunman could understand her. This was bad. He seemed to be getting aggravated. Sam allowed his power to flourish. He may need to act at any moment. Electricity began to generate around him, from his left index finger, up his back, down to his right index finger. He tried to lift his right arm and winced at the pain from the gunshot from earlier in the night.

Better relax on the right arm for this one. Just breathe.

Sam tended to talk to himself in moments of stress. A coping mechanism from when he was young that he couldn't quite shake. It had once been a way to keep the unruly energy inside him from flying off the handle, but now it was a habit that relaxed him in situations like this.

The gunman was getting impatient; he took the girl by the hair and brought her to her feet, tears flooding down her face.

"Someone is going to tell me how to shut off this goddamn alarm, or I'm putting a bullet in this girl's mouth!" The gunman's eyes widened.

Steady. Wait for your moment.

"You all think I'm messing with you!" The gunman cocked his weapon and looked around the room at the remaining three captives: A girl looking on, mouth bound, trying to plead with the gunner for mercy through the duct tape; one older man, trying to break free from his restraints; and the bank manager, doing his best to avoid eye contact.

Just wait for the shot.

The girl fought, with the gun in her mouth, to plead with the manager. He simply looked away.

The gunman forced her first to the other woman, bringing her and the gun inches from her face. "Do you know how to shut off the alarm?" The girl continued to cry and shake her head. He brought her over to the other man, who quickly stopped what he was doing as they approached.

"And you?" The man was brave, looking the gunman right in the eyes, face scrunched together in fury. The gunman didn't like that and took the gun out of the girl's mouth momentarily to smack him across the face with the butt of his weapon.

There must be a better vantage point I can get to.

Everywhere the gunman moved around the room, there was always something impeding his shot. Sam made his way around the room, finding it hard to find any sort of position where he wouldn't risk hurting a hostage. His lightning had always been a fickle power. He had some control, but once it left his hands, he could only point it in a general direction and hope it would obey. It was hard to hit a precise target—not impossible, but extremely difficult. It was almost as if it had a mind of its own, listening to him on certain days and acting unruly on others. Like in the theater earlier in the night, for instance, it had done what it was supposed to do. Granted, there had been far less collateral damage that could be caused there than here, but it behaved itself. Could he trust it to make a clear shot here?

The gunman was growing very angry now. He took the

girl over to the manager, the gun placed firmly to her head now so the entire room could hear her pleas for help. With one hand grasped to the back of her head, he forced her directly into the manager's face, who was continuing to look away. Sam was a little ways away, but he managed to set up behind the manager so that he could see the three of them. It was still too tight a shot; he would have to pray the lightning wouldn't clip either the manager or the girl before hitting his intended target.

Be patient Sam. The time will come.

"I'm getting sick of this. You are going to shut off this alarm on the count of three, or you are going to be covered in this girl's blood. Do you understand me?" The gunman remained behind the girl's head, making it difficult for Sam to find a shot.

You are running out of time, Sam!

"One!" The gunman yelled. The manager refused to look at the screaming girl.

If he just stood up a little, I could get the shot!

"Two!" The manager's head turned to meet the girl's, as if apologizing for what was about to happen.

Out of time, Sam!

"Three!" Before he could act, Sam jumped out of his hiding spot, sending a stream of lightning from his left hand. It managed to fly right by the manager's head, hitting the weapon out of the gunman's hand. He didn't, however, avoid the girl's face as she reeled back and fell to the floor. With the gunman unarmed however, Sam took the opportunity to close the distance. The gunman was obviously affected somewhat by the shot as he gripped his hand in pain, but upon seeing Sam he stood and reached around to the rifle at his back.

"Everyone down!" Sam screamed. The hostages hit the floor. He was close enough now, and with the gunman the only one in view, now his shot was sure to hit. He lifted his left hand again and shot a stream of lightning in his direction.

The familiar sight soon followed. The gunman's body seized up as the electricity passed through him. His eyes rolled to the back of his head, and he collapsed onto the ground. Without hesitation, Sam approached the downed gunman to check his pulse.

Still alive. Good.

He then proceeded to help the girl he had injured.

"Are you OK?" The girl had a deep gash across her face and was bleeding a lot. She was crying hysterically.

Way to go, Stormboy!

"I'll be right back, OK?" Sam had to help the others. He quickly untied the manager and the two other hostages. "Call an ambulance and get out of here right now!" The manager didn't waste any time leaving the building, while the other two stayed back to help the girl to her feet.

"Hey Stormboy," the male hostage called back to him. "There are three more guys inside."

"Thanks. Take care of her for me and . . ." He paused for a moment. "I'm sorry."

The three made their way out of the bank, thankfully. No more distractions. With three more criminals inside, Sam felt confident he could clean this up quickly. He allowed the electricity to surge around him. Letting it fly out violently like this appeased it somehow. It was almost like if he allowed it to be set free from time to time, it was more likely to obey him when the time came. He only wished he had done so earlier; maybe he wouldn't have hurt that girl. As much as that weighed on him, he had to persevere. He tried raising his right arm again and winced.

Better be careful.

With his right arm out of commission, it put a damper on his abilities. He had been able to fill an entire room with his power with access to both hands, but with just the one, single bolts would have to suffice. It was only three guys, after all. He thought about earlier in the night how the two guys in the theater were able to hurt him at full capacity, but he shrugged it off. Further, in there were three more bank robbers he needed to stop, and although there were no more hostages, he still needed to stay focused. Sam had a general idea of how the bank was laid out. There were points of interest he knew the robbers would be after to gain the most profit. With the bank siren still wailing in the background, there was no way they would hang around much longer. At least if they were smart. The vault had to be the first place to check. Sam made his way to the safe, making sure to be as cautious as possible. Taking moments to massage his right shoulder, he turned the corner to see the vault at the end of the hall partially open, but no one seemed to be around.

Maybe they heard me coming and ran.

Sam imagined the schematics of this building over and over in his head. There was no exit point between where the vault was and where he had walked into the building. Something else was going on here. He let his talent subside so he could listen for a moment. It would have to deal for a moment. The constant cracking and zapping of his powers only dulled his senses, and he needed to be entirely alert. He approached the heavy steel door and opened it. The room had a desk in the center and safety deposit boxes lining the walls from floor to ceiling, all of which were completely undisturbed. From what he could tell, everything was where it should be. Which could only mean one thing.

This is a trap!

Sam turned around to see two men, both with assault rifles homed in on the safe. There was no time to think. Sam quickly ran further into the safe and ducked behind the massive desk in the middle of the room moments before it was filled with bullets. He dove to the floor so suddenly he forgot about the injury on his right shoulder and landed right on top of it.

How could I be so stupid!

The bullets ricocheted all throughout the vault. Leaving

him on the floor, covering his head.

Think, Sam!

In the brief moments when the shooters were reloading, Sam could hear them shouting expletives. They had him pinned down.

"You just hang out right there, Stormboy. My boy will get what we need and be out of here before you know it!"

How did he let it get to this point? His mind raced to some sort of creed Freight Train had for something like this. But the sound of bullets striking metal kept interrupting him.

Breathe.

Sam took a moment to himself. He knew what he had to do. The bullets continued to fly through the vault, but he couldn't pay any attention to it. There was one way out of this, and it was to let his talent take over. He sat with his legs crossed and allowed the energy within him to flow. There was a joy that washed over him; he believed his talent had a certain influence over his mood, and being allowed to be let loose without any regard for anything else was exactly what it wanted. The shooters were still screaming, but Sam ignored it. Lightning filled the small room, lurching off him.

OK. Time to get us out of this.

He waited for a break in the gunfire. In the seconds between the changing of the clips, he revealed himself to his foes, slamming his hands down onto the floor. His power spread from his body down to his fingertips and out into the entire hall. It blanketed the floors, walls, and ceiling instantaneously. As the lightning made contact with the gunners, they convulsed violently. Sam witnessed their bodies twist and contort in agony. He didn't want to kill them. He would never intentionally do that, but he held his power longer than what may have been necessary. He really wanted them to feel this. He had finally released them from their torment, and they both fell with a thud onto the ground. As Sam made his way to his feet, he felt a slight feeling of ecstasy. He knew his ability liked to be unleashed in this manner—unrelenting, uncontrolled, and free. And when the lightning felt good, it made Sam feel good. He looked down at his hands where lightning still cracked and sparked, as if it was giddy to be used again. It would get its time. There was still one more criminal to take down.

Sam let out a violent scream that echoed through the halls of the bank. Whatever pain he had felt in his right arm didn't matter anymore. The rush of being Stormboy took him. He made his way back into the bank. He stopped momentarily to check to make sure the two he just took down were still breathing. It was slow, but they were breathing. That was good enough for him.

"I'm coming for you!" Stormboy screamed. Where else could this guy be? If the bank worker was to be trusted, then there should be one more! Stormboy did the only thing he could think of and made his way back toward the entrance. While navigating the back rooms of the bank, it didn't take him long to find the last man. He must have heard everything that happened to his team, because he was sitting with his arms hugging his knees, frozen in fear. Stormboy saw him, powers in a torrent, and knelt next to him.

"You know you're all alone now, right?" Stormboy whispered. The man nodded without bothering to look back at him. Sam loved this feeling. So many of these criminals subjugated the weak and the vulnerable; it felt right to throw it back at them. It was only fair. Someone had to put them in their place.

"You should give up now. We wouldn't want this to get any uglier." Stormboy picked up his weapon and with a burst of electricity sent it flying into hundreds of pieces. The man shuttered at the loud pop it made. He lifted him by the back of his shirt and guided him back toward the entrance, making sure to tie him up. He finally allowed his powers to subside. He was finally Sam again. As he approached the front of the bank, he could hear the wailing of police sirens, blended with the continued wail of the bank alarm.

Now they get here!

Upon making it outside, he was met with a flood of news cameras and reporters. Sam placed the now tied and subdued robber against the outer wall of the bank and made his escape. Reporters were always persistent in getting some sort of word out of him whenever they could, but that wasn't for Sam. Freight Train had loved all the attention, he would call the news cameras his "gateway" to address the citizens of Westside, but that wasn't Sam. Every time he stepped in front of those cameras, he needed to be Stormboy, the hero of Westside, but he couldn't help but to just be Sam, the frightened boy who just wanted to be left alone. As much as he would love to, Freight Train entrusted Westside to him—he had to be Stormboy. Whether he liked it or not, this was the reality. At the very least, he could avoid this aspect of it. As long as he protected the people of Westside, he wouldn't have to address them.

Sam escaped to a building top overlooking the exterior of the bank and just watched. He was far enough that no one could see him amongst the shadows of the rooftops but close enough to see all the people he had recently saved. That smug bank manager wasted no time talking to the news, getting front and center, enjoying all the attention, but it was the others Sam had really focused on. He watched as the others had family and friends come pick them up. Some exchanged hugs, others argued back and forth. All of which he knew was out of love. He lingered until the crowd dispersed. It was a pretty full night, Sam decided now would be as good a time as any to call it. The weird thing about heroism was knowing when to stop. Sam was sure if he stayed out on patrol he could easily stop another two or three crimes, but as Freight Train always said, "A man needs his rest."

It was a little way away from the bank, but he made his way to the "stash point." Freight Train and he had set up numerous stash points around the city, places that were hidden from prying eyes that they could store equipment and change of clothes as needed. Another of his mentor's mantras, "Never go home in uniform."

As he changed to his civilian clothes, he was reminded of the pain in his right arm. All the adrenaline faded, and he was back to not lifting his arm again.

Yeah. It's time to go home.

He expected the sun would be coming up any moment now, but as it was in Oldtown, there were still undesirables out. Sam did his best to avoid eye contact with anyone. He always took the most complicated route home just in case he was being followed. Sam's mind went through everything he had gone through tonight. It was more eventful than most, and where most people would be caught up in the fights he had or the injuries he had incurred, he couldn't help but think of the people. The kid in the theater caught up with the wrong crowd, or the bank employees just trying to do their jobs and how they all had someone to go home to, someone who cared about them.

Sam made his way to his apartment on the northeastern edge of Oldtown, doing his best not to wake his neighbors on the climb to the second floor. With a quick jiggle of his key, he opened the door to his home and was swiftly reminded of the state his life was in. He passed his kitchen with the sink piled with dishes he'd been telling himself for weeks he'd get to. Flies and other critters making their way with any food remaining on the plates and cups that were fit to overflow the rather small sink. Further in he passed his couch, illuminated by the TV he forgot to turn off, blanket sprawled out, undoubtedly covering some dirty clothes he has yet to pick up and take down to the laundromat. He ignored all the mess however, and made his way to his porch instead. He wished to ignore the disaster that was his personal life for just a little while longer.

On his balcony, he could hear the distant wails of sirens as the Westside police picked up the scraps of any criminals that Stormboy couldn't get to tonight. The noise comforted him, though. He couldn't stand the utter silence of his apartment. The weight of the responsibility of keeping his "Sam" life under control, all while being Stormboy as well. The noise from the outside drowned all of that out. He only had to be one thing, but those people he saved today made him wonder. The theater kid had his friend to go back to, and all the bank workers had their friends and family come claim them after their ordeal. Seeing the look on their faces as they were saved should've been enough. Then why did he feel so empty?

Suddenly, he heard a scream from a young lady. Sam looked down to the alley, and he noticed a man and a woman struggling to gain possession of a purse. Just when he thought his night was over. This girl had no idea how lucky she was!

You are the one who didn't want silence.

Sam leapt off the balcony and instinctually braced for his fall with his right hand flinching slightly upon hitting the floor. His sudden leap to the ground floor caught both the mugger and the girl off guard.

"OK, that's enough! Leave the poor girl alone," Sam shouted. They both looked at him quizzically, wondering where he had come from. During the confusion, the mugger gave one violent tug, freeing the purse from the young lady before sprinting in the opposite direction. Sam sighed; tonight had already been a full night—he really didn't want to engage in a chase! He began to pursue, regardless.

"Wait here!" Sam said as he passed the confused girl. Her face twisted in angry confusion. The mugger was doing all he could to escape Sam, twisting and turning down different corridors of the Westside streets. He had always described this city as a labyrinth of streets and alleys, but he's been navigating them for so long that they were his! It was only a matter of time before . . . bingo!

A fence had divided into two alleyways, forcing the mugger to scale it before resuming his escape. This gave Sam, or Stormboy, plenty of time to line his shot. He extended his left index finger with thumb pointed upward. His power began to flourish down his arm until it reached his finger. As soon as the mugger made it to the other side of the fence, Stormboy plunged his finger down, letting loose a single bolt that sailed through the fence and directly into the mugger's back, knocking him clear off his feet. If it hadn't been for all the running, this would've been Sam's easiest job ever. He scaled the fence after him, reclaiming the purse, and began to head back to the girl. Much to his surprise, as soon as he reached the main road she was there, completely out of breath.

Did she really try to follow him?

He handed her the purse as she struggled to find words to thank him.

"You're welcome," he said to her, relieving her of the burden of speaking, and handed her the bag. "This is a rough part of town. You probably shouldn't be out here so late."

Sam gave her a slight wave before making his way back home. Tonight had been eventful enough. It was time for him to head back home. He thought he might have heard something from the girl, but it was stolen by the streets of Westside.

CHAPTER 2

INTRUDER

Sam had awoken to furious banging. How long had it been? He looked over to his clock next to the couch.

9:00 a.m.?

It was earlier than he had seen in years. Nights as Stormboy didn't really lend themselves to early mornings like this. All sorts of scenarios ran through his head.

Did I forget the rent? It could be some religious freak trying to pass on the "good word."

He tried to fight off the incessant noise, but to no avail. Frustrated, Sam brought himself to his feet and made himself presentable.

"Hang on, I'm coming!" He approached the door; the noise, once just an annoying garble of banging and muted tones, became more and more comprehensible. He could hear the argument his neighbors were having just on the other side of the door.

What am I walking into here?

Sam swung the door open to the ensuing conflict. The sweet old Spanish lady, Senora Ortiz, let out a series of words he couldn't quite understand, but between her facial expression and her wagging finger, Sam knew she was not thrilled with the commotion so early in the morning. His other neighbor, a fit man with dark black skin and a thick long braid running down to his lower back, was clutching a baseball bat at his unwanted guest.

This could get messy!

Sam had to do something! He turned to his intruder and was suddenly struck. She had long, perfectly straight hair, which became a lighter and lighter brown as it fell from her head to the point where it settled on her shoulders. Her eyes, although tight with intensity, were a soothing caramel color Sam could get lost in. Her lips, thick and pink with shades of what must have been the lipstick she had on the night before, were contorting into rebuttals against the verbal assault she was receiving from Sam's neighbors.

Right—the argument!

Sam snapped back into reality; there was mediation he needed to attend to.

"Mrs. Ortiz, Darius. Please calm down. I'm here now; I'm so sorry!"

"You better get your girl, Sammy! Way too early for this." Darius seemed thoroughly upset, which was understandable. Judging by his tank top and loose fitted pants, he was woken up from sleep. Despite the weapon he looked keen on using, he was generally harmless. He was probably just concerned for his two girls inside.

"Mijo! You can't have people making so much noise so early!"

"I know, and I'm sorry. I got it now. OK?"

"I'm not doing anything wrong. I'm allowed to be here," the beautiful woman said. She wasn't going to make this easy, it seemed. Senora Ortiz gave a look to the girl and then one to Sam before muttering something else he couldn't quite catch. At least she was heading back inside. Darius had also relaxed his bat swinging arm, and decided to head inside as well, leaving Sam with his intruder.

"May I help you?" Sam finally addressed his guest. He had

a hard time getting those words out as he adjusted his gaze to her.

"Hi!" she sang out jubilantly. She was full of so much energy! "I brought breakfast."

Sam looked at her hand and, sure enough, there was a bag filled with doughnuts and bagels.

"OK, why though?" Sam replied, clearly confused.

"I wasn't sure what you liked, so I kind of just got a bunch of everything."

It was as if she didn't even hear him as she dug through her bag. She finally turned to him again. "Can I come in?"

Unsure whether it was her intoxicating enthusiasm, or if it was the fact that Sam had been up at such an ungodly hour, he gestured for her to come inside.

"I wanted to thank you for . . ." before she could finish, she was witness to the state of his home. Sam followed her inside and was met with her sudden stop in the middle of the hallway. He squeezed his way past her.

"Thank me for what?" Sam couldn't quite put his finger on where he knew this girl from.

"This place is a mess!" She shoved the bag into Sam's hands and rolled up her sleeves. Sam, caught off guard yet again, cleared room off his table and placed the bag down.

"You know you really don't have to."

What did I do?

Sam had chased her from one side of the apartment to another as she threw things out and passed her hand over some neglected shelves to clear a thick coat of dust.

"I just want to know why you're here," Sam continued.

"Oh please, don't worry about it. This is the least I could do."

What is she talking about?

"Just sit there and eat your food. Let me do this."

There was a serenity to her voice that put Sam at ease. He didn't even know her, but it felt as if he could trust her. Despite the fire she had just a moment ago dealing with his neighbors, he felt relaxed now around her. He finally gave in and allowed her to continue. He watched intently as she scoured his apartment for anything she could use to clean up. Her eyes furrowed, and her lips puckered as she dove into his cabinets. Surprisingly, she was able to find some stuff even he wasn't aware he had. Sam couldn't take his eyes off her. She was nimble and resourceful. He was embarrassed to realize that maybe he had been staring at her for a little too long as she scrubbed the kitchen counter. Their eyes met momentarily, and she gave a quick smirk, which caused Sam to retreat into his donut, finding anything else his eyes could focus on.

What is happening right now?

Several moments passed, and she sighed triumphantly. Sam noticed that the kitchen had a lot more space than he had remembered suddenly.

"OK, now to the rest of it." She began walking to the living room before Sam stopped her.

"Can you please just relax for a minute and talk to me?" Sam led her to a seat on the couch next to him.

"But . . ." she looked on at the rest of the apartment anxiously but reluctantly sat.

"Have a donut." She looked as if Sam had insulted her, staring at him through the side of her face.

"I want the everything bagel," Sam sighed, shoving the donut in his mouth before reaching in and handing her the requested bagel.

"Don't get me wrong," Sam began, as he wanted to take advantage of the unusually calm state she was in. "Thank you for doing this, but why?"

"Well, you saved me last night. It's the least I can do for the great Stormboy!"

It was like one of his own lightning bolts struck his heart. Sam had to relax, though; his next words were important.

How could she know? Have I met her before?

He began to cycle through any moment in his past where

his disguise may have been compromised.

"I'm sorry—Stormboy?" Sam tried to stay as coy as possible. He had to feed into any iota of doubt she may still have.

"Yeah, you know, vigilante. Shoots lightning from his fingertips, saves girls' purses from robbers in alleys behind his house. Stormboy . . . you!" She took another bite of her bagel and smiled.

"But how can you make that leap in logic like that? I . . ."

"Don't bother. I saw you leap from your balcony and come to my rescue."

How could I show her where Stormboy lives?

"I followed you as you chased that guy and stopped him with your . . . zappy thing!" She made the same motion as he had last night, pointing her finger at him and plunging her thumb down before pretending to be struck by the bolt. Sam was stunned.

What do I do?

He could feel Mr. Kain's words running though his head; he combed through years of lessons, digging for one that was relevant.

Everything for them. Stay calm! Rushing leads to mistakes. Mistakes cost lives.

Nothing! All these words and nothing about this!

"Thank you." The words slipped from his mouth.

Why did I say that?

"Like I said, it's the least I could do," she replied as she leaned forward and placed her hand on his. Sam immediately took his hand back and buried his face in it.

"Are you OK, Stormboy?" Sam went to cover her mouth but winced at the sudden exertion; his arm was still in pain from last night. A look of concern flashed across her face.

"Can you please stop saying that so loudly?" Sam knew the walls weren't the thickest, and Senora Ortiz could be extremely nosy at times.

"I'm sorry." She placed her hands over her mouth as if

finally realizing what she had done. "This must be really weird for you."

Sam massaged his shoulder.

"Can I see?" she pointed at the place where Sam was clutching. He looked at her, concerned, but there was something in her eyes. A sincerity he had never seen in anyone before—it left him defenseless. She peaked down his shirt to the blood-soaked gauze he had taped to his arm.

"We should probably change this," she said, removing the padding and exposing the wound beneath.

"I have a kit in . . ."

"I know where it is," she interrupted. Sam, realized she had literally gone through all his stuff just moments before, of course she knew where the kit was. She returned with a cloth and fresh bandage. "You would think you would know how to clean a wound better."

Sam wanted to respond, but before he could, he gasped as the wet rag touched the wound.

"Sorry." She winced along with him.

"How could I be so stupid?" Sam slapped his face with his good hand.

"No! You aren't stupid!" she said. She finished wrapping up the arm. "I'm just observant. My mom used to have to iron my clothes three times before sending me to school because I could always see a wrinkle she missed."

"What?" Sam peaked out from behind his hand. He couldn't process what she was saying.

"Um . . ." She was nervous. For the first time since they'd met, she was struggling to find words. She could've probably yelled at Darius all day long, but when it came to this, she was getting flustered.

"It's no big deal," she continued. "I swear, I'm really good at keeping secrets, and if there is anything that you need help with, well I guess I can do that. I'll do anything, just please don't be upset at me!"

He lowered his hand from his face. She carried a sincere smile that hid a guilt that her eyes gave away. She was remarkable. She had pushed her slender shoulders together, her arms shoved into her legs, guarding her body. The light from his only window made it seem like she sat there on purpose. It caught about a third of her that made pieces of her brown hair illuminate so bright it looked like a different shade entirely. His eyes lingered just long enough; he could tell it was getting awkward.

What do I say?

Mr. Kain wasn't going to like this. All his lessons kept screaming in his head, now that he had regained focus on the situation. It was only him now. No longer a sidekick. He knew he had to act.

"OK," he said. He wiped his face with an effort to throw away any sort of angst he was feeling. He turned to her. "So, you know who I am. Fine. You said you won't say anything, great. Thank you for everything, but you have to go. Now!" It was the only way to keep them both safe.

"But I'm not done cleaning," she said as she began tidying up again. It was a nervous tick she needed to satisfy.

"Listen," Sam said sternly. He had remembered when Mr. Kain had to get a point across to him, and the tone he took. "You even being here is dangerous. My honest opinion is, and I highly recommend it, forget you ever saw me, and move on with your life." It didn't sound like him, hell it didn't feel like him. Sam puffed his chest and kept his serious expression the whole time, but it felt forced and phony. It didn't matter, though; it was for her own good.

"But how?" she said. She still wasn't getting it. This wasn't the way it had gone in his head.

"What do you mean?" Sam said. "You just get your things and leave."

"And what about you?"

"What about me? I'll be fine."

"Nope, not good enough. Someone has to tidy this place up."

Who was this woman? Why wouldn't she just listen to him? She began cleaning again while Sam stood there in shock. He felt as if the only option left was to pick her up and literally toss her out. It was a tempting thought, but now of all times Mr. Kain's lessons came to him: *disrespecting women in any capacity is the worse crime of all!* If only Mr. Kain had met this particular woman, maybe he would've changed his mind. She wouldn't stay still. Every time Sam tried to interject and tell her to stop, she went off to another corner to clean something else. It was exhausting. So, he did the only thing he knew to do and collapsed back on his couch and let out another heavy sigh.

"So . . . Stormboy," she said, after a few minutes of cleaning. Sam had sat with his eyes closed, facing skyward, massaging his temples.

"Please don't call me that. No one else needs to find out my secret. Besides, I hate that name."

"You should probably tell the papers then, because they seem to love it!"

She wasn't wrong. He had stopped the bank robbery last night. He was sure that name would be in bold lettering across all the newspapers in town.

"But fine. What do I call you then?"

"Samual," he said, "but people usually call me Sam. It's easier."

"Well, I'm not going to do that, Samual." It's like you could never predict what she was going to say. Sam began to doubt everything Mr. Kain had told him about women. "My name is Samantha, and everyone calls me Sam, so that's not going to work. So, I'll just call you Samual."

"How about I call you by your name and you call me Sam?" She took a second to think about it.

"Naw, I think we should do it my way," She giggled. "Besides, I really like that name. .. Samual." She paused for emphasis as she framed with her fingers in a way to picture his name in the sky. All these years Samual had hated his name, but she made it sound different. Like it was OK. Sam or Samual, as long as it wasn't Stormboy.

"So why do you hate the name Stormboy so much?" she asked.

"I never liked it. When I was Freight Train's side . . ." He stopped himself. "partner, he said the press needed a name, so he gave it to me. I did what I was told, and I was stuck."

"So, what do you want to be called?"

He'd never thought about it before. Freight Train gave him the name, and that was always what it was going to be.

"It really doesn't matter. As long as I'm able to do what I do, they can call me what they want."

"So how about Lightning Lad or the Electric Elite?"

"Please, stop."

She had been enjoying herself too much at his expense.

"So, you can control electricity, right?" She had a filthy rag she was wringing nervously in her hands. This had become an interrogation, but he didn't mind. It was foreign to him to open up this way to someone, and for some reason, despite her eccentric nature, he felt calm with her.

"Yes."

"Can I see?" The rag twisted as far as it could, and she let a smile leap on her face. Samual felt like a sideshow attraction but was also afraid to disappoint her.

"Stand back." He reluctantly rose to his feet and pressed his hands together, as if beginning a prayer. He had to concentrate. If he lost control for a second, he could really hurt her, but it was a spectacle he was eager to show. His ability began to surge. It sparked and flashed all around the room, ricocheting off the corner of his apartment. He had to shut his eyes for the most part to concentrate, but he managed to peek a little to see her reaction. Her mouth was agape in silent amazement. Her neck whipped around as she tried to follow each streak that zipped through the air.

Perfect!

Occasionally, she would giggle as the static filled the room, which caused her hair to flail out in all different directions. She did everything she could to keep herself together, and Samual couldn't take his eyes off her. One strand of lightning, however, strayed a little too close, and Samantha gasped as it sparked against her arm.

"I'm so sorry!" he exclaimed. Samual completely shut his power down and went to her side.

"Wow!" She laughed, clutching her arm where she was shocked. "That was amazing!"

"Are you OK?" Samual approached to inspect her arm.

"Please, I'm fine," she replied. She moved her hand aside, showing a slight redness on her skin.

"I really shouldn't have used my powers like that. I've never done anything like that before." Samual remembered back to his training and how dangerous his abilities could be and all the work Mr. Kain had done with him to avoid this very situation. He could see him now in his head, scolding him for using his powers in such an irresponsible manner. Samantha approached him and tried to touch him, cautiously, as if he were radioactive. It was a strange mix of curiosity and fear. It was an expression that Samual was quite familiar with.

"I scare you, don't I?" he asked. She noticed what he said and finally touched his shoulder. A spark clipped her finger, and she jumped back.

"No," she said, straightening herself out. "Sorry, it's just . . . wow, you know?"

She was being nice. Samual thought back to his mother's expression when he exhibited his ability for the first time, or the foster family that tried to raise him in her place. That look always made him weary. This is why the only person who ever understood him was Mr. Kain. He saw Samual in a way the rest of the world never could. He wasn't just a spectacle to him. He stepped back from Samantha, and a silence lingered between them.

"I should go," she said, turning to grab her purse.

I should've done this sooner.

Who would've thought this was all he needed to do to get her to leave?

Be yourself. That ought to send them running.

She was close to the door now, and Samual couldn't help but feel he had done something wrong. He ran his hands down his face as he followed her silently. The walk to the front door felt like an eternity. He had never been in this situation before. What should he say? Before he could think about it any further, Samantha turned to meet him.

"Thank you." Her eyes met his toes, and she found the courage to push them to his face. "I owe you my life."

"No, just your purse."

She didn't budge. She had opened the door behind her and made her way outside. How could it be that such an ordinary experience threw him for such a loop? More of Mr. Kain's proverbs echoed in his head— "*A man needs his rest to operate effectively.*" He felt his eyes getting heavy from the lack of sleep. She began to exit. The moment was over, and he wasn't sure how exactly he felt. Nothing his mentor had ever said prepared him for this. He clutched the door to close it behind her.

"I haven't finished the living room yet. If I come back another time," she continued to speak, but he couldn't hear her anymore.

"You would come back?"

"Of course. I promised I would do this for you. That would be OK, right?"

The door was halfway closed now, and Samual hid behind it, like a scared child who had just been scolded.

Why does she want to come back? She saw me! I can end this now. Save her from me.

"Maybe." Samual quickly shut the door, leaving them both

alone on opposite sides of the door. He walked back inside his apartment. He looked around at the newly cleaned environment. It didn't feel like his anymore. He was tired. He made his way to his couch and collapsed.

A man needs his rest.

CHAPTER 3

EIGHT YEARS AGO

Samual didn't enjoy being out so late. It was something Mr. Kain told him he had to start getting used to. It was less the time, and more the area. The flickering streetlights and the dozens of night dwellers who stood around gazed at Sam, recognizing him as an outsider. He knew it; he could feel their cold stares trickle up and down his spine. Sam had his hood up and his mask on, full sidekick attire, which for these people posed an issue. Mr. Kain, or "Freight Train," as he reminded himself to call him tonight, never left him alone like this before. He was sixteen! How could he just leave him here like this?

"Show no fear to these people. They will sense it, they will act, and you will hurt them." Freight Train's sermons rang in his head. He had the power to kill anyone that came across him, but that hadn't made him better. It was this thought, Freight Train told him, that separated himself from everyone else. It was Samual's first time on a real mission, and he didn't want to disappoint his mentor.

He took a deep breath and composed himself. The most important exercise was to breathe. He wondered if he still had thoughts for himself or if he was merely an extension of

Mr Kain. He couldn't dwell on this any longer. He had to focus on the plan. The streets were surprisingly devoid of cars. Sam had never seen this part of town so deserted; it must have had something to do with the tip they had received earlier in the week. A major gang boss was meeting with a drug supplier. Freight Train would bust up the deal and should the criminals escape, the only way out was through the street where Sam would be. As much as Sam prayed, it didn't come to that. He knew Mr. Kain would not have asked him out there if there wasn't a good chance that he was needed.

Everything for them!

The roar of some engines came echoing down the street so loud the ground was shaking. The lightning began to ring out of control from his body, much like his heart beating out of his chest. His vision dimmed as his anxiety heightened. Two cars peeled out from around the corner. He wasn't ready! Tears began to flood his face, and his power, which he had trained so long to maintain, raged out of his control. Window and streetlamps shattered, and those same night dwellers who had given him a look before, now ran and hid in fear of the storm they found themselves in. The cars drew closer and closer, and Sam had realized his mentor was hanging from the side of one of the cars. His immense strength allowed him to latch onto the passenger side door, despite it swerving all over the road. Sam watched his mentor's bravery and couldn't help but be ashamed of his own cowardice. But how could he not be scared? He wasn't ready for this! The vehicles came careening down the road, revving and swerving desperately to shake loose the hero's hold. It was then Sam heard a familiar voice call out.

"Do it!" Freight Train called out. "Do it now!"

Sam jumped to the middle of the road on Freight Train's command, and with his soaking face and rattled nerves, he slammed both his electrically charged hands firmly on the ground. Sam's power gleefully leaped across the street. As it whizzed past the cars, it blew out all eight tires, causing them to flip straight over his head and crash further down the road before coming to a complete stop. Sam refused to open his eyes during the duration of the experience and only managed to open them when the scraping of metal against pavement finally ceased. He allowed the silence to take hold for a few seconds before opening his eyes and witnessing what he had done. One car had sat completely upside down, and the other on its side with his mentor standing triumphantly on top. Freight Train pulled open the doors to wrangle up all the guilty parties inside.

Did I do it?

It was then he looked around to see his collateral damage. Those night dwellers, who had looked suspiciously at him earlier, had every right to be scared. Some were sprinting away as if they had just heard gunshots. They were the lucky ones. Others shook violently on the ground as the electricity surged through their bodies. Guilt overwhelmed him. Who should he help? Should he join his mentor or confront the ones he hurt?

"Stormboy!" His mentor's screams hit him like a slap in his back, and his choice was made for him. He sprinted as fast as he could, face securely toward the ground. Sam wanted nothing more than for this night to be over.

"I'm here, mister . . ." He caught himself before he could ruin things further. Freight Train gave him a stern look. "Sorry. Freight Train."

Freight Train's expression softened momentarily before witnessing the carnage Sam had caused.

"What did we say about control?"

Sam's face flushed, and his head sank lower than he thought possible. He felt small, and wondered if the criminals they were apprehending could hear the punishment he was getting. Freight Train realized what he had done and handed Sam his cell phone.

"This is the big time now, Stormboy. I need you to listen to me! I'm going to go tend to the bystanders, call an ambulance and don't let this guy out of your sight."

Sam raised his head just long enough to grab the phone.

"Stormboy!"

"Yes, sir."

"Good. If any of them try to escape, don't hold back." Freight Train ran off like the hero once more, leaving Sam alone.

Why am I out here? I'm not ready!

Sam dialed the phone for an emergency vehicle, when out of the corner of his eye, he spotted a man clawing his way out of the car and onto his feet, and for a moment their eyes met.

"9-1-1. What's your emergency?" His heart stopped. They stared at each other, and it was clear that no one knew exactly how to act. The criminal began to limp in the opposite direction, gathering all his strength to do so but not getting very far.

"9-1-1?"

Sam stared at the hobbling man. His electricity built without his command.

"We are going to need an ambulance."

CHAPTER 4

NORMAL

"Stop, Tony!" Stormboy shouted, but the hoodlum persisted. "I really don't want to do this!" This was his least favorite part of the job, the chase; they always ran! It had been early enough in the night that there were still people out on the streets, so as much as he would've wanted to snipe this guy and call it a day, he couldn't risk it with so many people around. The two of them ducked and dodged their way through downtown Westside.

Drugs had always been a problem in Westside, one that he and Freight Train had been fighting for years together to keep under control. It had gotten a lot better, but there were still hoods like Tony running around. He had once been a low-rate dealer, but as the years went on, he'd gotten something of a reputation and employed kids like Anton to push his product. He had been caught and put in prison three times, but guys like him always managed to sneak through the cracks of the system somehow.

"Get away from me! I ain't going back in the box!" Tony shouted back at him before turning a corner down another street. Stormboy had bigger things to worry about, like that girl. She had seen him for what he was, and he just let her go!

For all he knew, the news was displaying a full report on him now.

"This just in! Stormboy identity revealed. Latest damsel tells all about the idiot scourge of Westside who saves her without his mask on!"

It felt, as he was running through the crowd, that everyone was whispering to each other about the juicy new gossip they just got.

Focus, Sam!

He turned the corner; he was lucky. Tony looked as if he had tripped and fallen over a group of friends. He quickly got to his feet and continued running once he saw Stormboy.

Would she really do something like that? Who are you kidding Sam, who wouldn't? You're a freak who's hurt just as many people as you've saved.

As much as he couldn't avoid thinking about it, he also remembered for a moment when his powers had flourished, and she had that look of amazement in her eyes. Her sweet smile had warmed everything inside him, making him feel more than just Samual or Stormboy.

Tony had been shouting things back at him the entire time, but he didn't bother trying to make it out. This was the standard dance between the two of them. Tony would run, he would tire himself out, thinking he could outrun him on his streets and as always, he would get caught. They had been playing this game for years now. It was only a matter of time. Sam recognized the familiar look of Oldtown. He must have been running for a good while now.

He must be running back to his hideout.

"All right, it's time to stop this, Tony. I'm giving you a chance to surrender." He responded with a middle finger before adjusting himself and rushing down a narrow alleyway. Stormboy sighed heavily, but this was his chance. He could finally let his powers out without fear of civilians getting caught up in the fury. Oldtown didn't have people hanging around like that, not this early, anyway. Stormboy turned down the alley to follow him when something struck him in the face. He hit the ground hard and fast. Tony and two others were pelting him with wooded bats and fists. He put his hands up in defense, but he couldn't be everywhere. He would catch the bat, but a fist would come down on his shoulder or his gut, forcing him to release it. He writhed and contorted in agony. Every effort he made to guard himself just left another area open for more abuse. His vision went dark.

I can't believe I let them get the drop on me.

His mind swam in the darkness, and for some reason his first family came to mind. The Williamses, an older couple who weren't able to have children of their own. They often spoke about how they would travel and all the interesting monuments they saw on their numerous trips around the world. He had been so used to the rundown buildings in the projects of Westside that seeing the intricate skyscrapers, such as the Chrysler Building in New York City or the pointed peaks of the Sydney Opera House in Australia, opened his eyes to a new realm of imagination. The world had seemed so small in Westside, but there was so much to see and discover. His favorite, however, had been the Taj Mahal. The beautiful towers and domed roofs gave it a unique elegance like Samual had never seen before. An entire structure was built to the memory and love of the emperor's wife! Every single place in the world was a stamp of creative cultural architecture, each its own. Mr. Williams had shown him so much, he truly felt he found a home and a family he could be with forever.

But there was no such thing as forever for Samual. It was only a matter of time. Even though he had tried so hard to make sure it wouldn't happen. He couldn't have been any older than six at the time, his powers were wildly out of control. He maintained some handle on it by sneaking out at night and discharging as much electricity from his body in hopes it would not overwhelm him during the day. One day he got caught sneaking out of his bedroom window and was forced to remain inside. Samual begged and pleaded, but he was too young, and it was too late. He remembered crying all night. His power rained out of him with a vengeance. It was a clear statement from it, telling him, "You can't have a normal life, not now, not ever!" Scars from lighting strikes tore apart his childhood room, and the Williamses, from then on, were too scared of what he was to keep him. He couldn't quite remember what the Williamses sounded like, but the memory of them and the words they spoke to him that night he could never forget. "Monster."

After a time, he opened his eyes as much as he could. The moon stared back at him, looming over the alleyway. He reached to touch his face. His ears and nose were rivers of blood. He had to push himself to sit up. There they were, both of them, all laid out on the floor.

Of course Tony got away!

He went over to them. Only one of them was breathing.

Not again.

It hadn't been the first time something like this happened. His powers acted as a defense mechanism. It would react out of self-preservation all the time. It was fortunate for Samual, not so much for everyone else.

"Hey! You OK?" Stormboy sat the one who made it up and lightly slapped him on the face. He moaned weakly. Stormboy found whatever strength he could and bound the one still alive with some spare rope he carried on him and left them for someone to come pick up.

Freight Train would have never allowed himself to be jumped like he was. He could feel the blood seep in from a cut inside his mouth. He spat it out in anger while changing back into his civilian clothes. As much as he wanted to continue, being Stormboy had to end here tonight. A monumental amount of shame washed over him.

What if someone else had been around? What if they managed to jump you downtown?

The thought frightened him. As if the public didn't fear him enough already. Freight Train's words wouldn't leave his head the whole walk home.

"You need to be better!"

The next morning, Samual woke to his body beaten and broken. He took his time to roll off his sofa and stumbled his way to the bathroom. The vision in the mirror was horrifying. The bruises on his face and shoulders made him look like a ripe plum.

How much longer can he keep this up?

He washed his face in the faint hope some of his original color would return, but it was interrupted by a scraping at the door. It was barely audible. Samual had to shut off the water just to make sure there wasn't a problem with the sink. As he approached the door, he could make out a faint whisper. Cautiously, he opened the door, making sure the lock chain held tight.

"I didn't want your crazy neighbors to yell at me again." It was that girl! She wore an old white tank top with a bright teal sports bra underneath. Barely stretched over her hips were a pair of denim shorts that stopped on her upper thigh, leaving the fullness of her legs on display.

"What are you doing here?" Sam asked. Pressed against her hip was a basket filled with chemicals and sprays.

"I told you I wasn't done yet. I still owe you." She kept her voice low but had that same bubbly smile and bounced around as if she was preparing to jump onto the floor above them. She only started to relax when the silence between them began to linger.

"So, are you going to let me in?" she said. Samual realized he had a lump growing in the back of his throat.

"Um. One second." He undid the latch on the door, and she exploded in as soon as she was able.

"A promise is a promise," she said, turning to him. She caught an actual look at him for the first time since she arrived. "Oh my God! What happened to your face?"

"Occupational hazard." He lightly touched his face where he felt it pulsing. "It's . . ."

"Did you ice it? You look like you were hit by a truck!" she interrupted. Samantha grabbed him by his wrist and pulled him toward his kitchen. She wrapped some ice in some paper towels and placed it gently against his face.

"Do you always get beat up like this?"

"Sometimes." Samual wondered why he felt so ashamed. Her expression was one he hadn't seen in a while. It was pity. "It's fine. I'm fine, just a few bumps and bruises. No big deal!"

"Whatever you say big guy." She tilted the towel back to get another look and her face twisted. "Keep that there for a bit; it'll help the swelling."

She gave him the ice and turned back to get her materials.

"Welp, I guess it's time to get started." She clapped her hands together, preparing for the daunting task she had ahead of her, and before Samual could ask her anything, she was off. Had she said anything to anyone about the last time she was there? Sam had so many questions, but it was too late. She was a spectacle of efficiency. She popped open a garbage bag and went to town. Before long, it started to resemble the place it was when he first got it. She had a tool for everything. Stains Samual once thought were permanent, washed away with ease. It was an elegant dance she did across his tiny place, and everything she touched was returned to pristine condition. Much like the first time he had met her, she was a force of nature. Trying to wrangle her to have any sort of meaningful interaction seemed futile. Even though one of his eyes was covered, she was a marvel to behold. She had her hair pulled back into a short ponytail. Samual preferred it this way, as her long hair no longer passed in front of her beautiful face. He even loved how her cheeks began to redden as the toll of work began to become more and more difficult.

Stop it! She knows your secret! You must find out who she told.

He wanted to dislike her. She was the sole person in the world that could ruin everything. Her mere existence was in violation of the code. But every time he looked at her, he found it hard to hate her. Especially since she would occasionally look at him and let out a deep sigh of exhaustion, blowing up the loose strands of hair that had gotten on her face before smiling and winking at him. The action immobilized him, and he would forget momentarily why he was so upset at her to begin with.

"Woosh. That was rough!" Samantha exhaled. The place looked brand new. Samual had helped her move some trash to the dumpster, but otherwise she had turned this place around all on her own. She had gone to the sink to wash her face. She sighed a gleeful sigh as the cool water hit her face, and Sam knew this was the only time he'd have to ask.

"Did you tell anyone?"

"Tell anyone what?"

Sam's eyes thinned. "Don't play dumb. Did you tell anyone what I am?"

Samantha giggled, seeing how much this was irritating him. "No. Of course not. Why would I?" she asked. Samual could think of several reasons. "Besides, who would I tell?"

Does she really think nothing of this?

She had to have known this was important to him.

"I wasn't expecting to work so hard." She aired her shirt out against her chest. "You wouldn't mind if I used your bathroom to freshen up?"

"Sure, not a problem." He wanted to direct her to the proper place, but she was already halfway there before he had a chance. Figures, she had just finished cleaning it, of course she knew where it was.

Sam gave her privacy and went to the balcony to cool off. The alley was abandoned as usual. He remembered that night that started all of this, Samantha struggling to retrieve her purse from that jerk. He thought how easy it would have

47

been to rush back inside and grab his mask before leaping into action that night.

She still would've seen you leap from your balcony. She would've known where you lived, regardless.

He replayed the scenario repeatedly in his head, trying to think of something that would have saved him from all this. No teachings or gospel Freight Train taught prepared him for this. The ice had practically melted away against his face, and Sam tossed it to the ground.

"This is how your house gets the way it is, you know." Samantha's voice caught him by surprise. "Pick that up!"

Reluctantly he obeyed. He felt bad, she just spent all this time helping him clean.

"Sorry."

The two sat and stared into the alley.

"Ahh, memories," she said, which made them both laugh.

"Thank you," Samual managed to say. "You could've gone to anyone and spilled my secret, but you came here and helped me instead." Samual felt utterly confused. Anyone else in his life would have sold him out. Called him a freak or monster and been done with him. But she stayed.

"Your face is already looking a lot better." She touched where he had his ice moments earlier. "You are starting to look like Sam again."

"I thought you were Sam."

"I think I can let go of the name for the hero of Westside." She let out an exaggerated sigh. "You better be grateful."

"I am," he smiled. "I really don't like the name Samual."

"You don't like Samual, you don't like Stormboy, what do you like?"

Words caught in Sam's throat. All he could do was smile.

"So, what made you leap off your balcony despite it all to save little ol' me?" she said, eyes fluttering.

"It's what I do. It's what I was taught to do." His response felt programmed. He'd asked himself the same question over and over again, and the same response always came to him. It was burned into his identity. Being Stormboy took precedence over everything, always.

"So, you didn't see a pretty young girl getting robbed. You saw a crime that needed stopping?"

"I guess." He didn't know how else to phrase it. Samantha's lips twisted.

"I see," she said calmly. Sam's eyes remained focused on the alley while Samantha's roamed the rest of the patio, both determined not to look at the other. "Well, little ol' me could use an escort home if you are willing to work as a civilian."

"You're leaving?" he asked a little more concerned than he had meant to lead on.

"Why yes, Samual. My life doesn't revolve around you. But who knows what dangers Westside has in store for me. I need the great Stormboy to protect me!"

Samual's eyes quickly darted around to make sure no one was in earshot.

"Shh! You don't know who's listening!"

"Oh please, I don't think I'll be able to make it home without the protection of the great and powerful Stormboy! Whose real name is . . ."

Sam leapt up and covered her mouth with both his hands.

"Ok fine! I'll walk you home, just stop talking so loudly!" Samantha let out a muffled squeal of satisfaction before kissing his palm which caused him to pull away swiftly.

"Great!" she exclaimed. "I'll grab my stuff."

She rushed back into the house with Samual following behind. What did she want? Who would be so selfish? He couldn't wrap his head around her.

"You ready?" She stood with her basket of supplies, smiling intently.

"Yeah," he responded. He took the basket from her hands, as that was what Freight Train always taught him to do.

"Never let a woman carry something while our hands are

empty!" The mantra came back to him instinctually.

Did Mr. Kain ever have to deal with this kind of thing?

They walked side by side down the city streets. The simple task seemed harder now than it ever had before.

Am I standing too close? Maybe I should slow and match her speed better. Stand up straight! You're slouching. What is that smell, is that me?

He had been berating himself for so long he had forgotten that he should be engaging with her. Samantha paid him no mind, however. She had been majestic in every aspect, even her walk seemed like she was less stepping and more floating like an angel.

"So how long have you lived in Westside?" It was the only small talk question he had, and he prayed it would carry him the entire trip.

"About four months now. I try not to make it a point to stay in one place for too long," she said. "The world is such a big place it would be a crime not to experience it all if you can."

"Yeah, I guess so," Sam replied. "I've never really been anywhere else other than here, so I really wouldn't know."

"So why don't you go?"

"The job really doesn't allow for travel like that. I have a duty to the city."

"You think so?" Samantha stopped for a moment in front of a newspaper kiosk. The paper headline read, "Another Citizen Killed by Westside Vigilante." Samual turned away.

"Seems like they don't care too much whether you save them or not. Did you really kill that guy?" she asked nervously.

"They jumped me, and my body kind of just reacted." Sam wanted to shock the entire news stand. They didn't know what happened.

"Hey. It's OK. I understand," Samantha replied. "But you see my point, right?"

"Doesn't matter. Doesn't change the duty. We don't do it for people to like us. We do it to keep people safe." The soul-crushing reality always hurt. It was all cursed, and unless people miraculously stopped hurting and stealing from each other, he was stuck doing this for the rest of his life. Just like Freight Train before him.

"OK, but if you could go anywhere in the world, where would it be?"

"The Taj Mahal," Samual said, without any hesitation.

"Oh wow! Big aspirations! Any reason in particular?" Before he could answer, a chime came from her pocket. "Oh, no!"

"Is everything OK?"

"I'm so sorry, Sam, but I have to go." She pulled her belongings from Sam's hand. He wanted to say something, but like always, she was everywhere at once, and he couldn't pin her down. "Good-bye! Thanks for walking me this far!"

Before he could even respond to her, she was gone. He couldn't help but laugh. It was so typical of her. When he thought things were one way, she'd pull the rug out from under him and make it something else entirely. It had been strange though, now that she was gone, there was so much he wanted to say. All these thoughts he had never dreamed of thinking before. The thought of leaving Westside felt selfish at best. His job was here. But the minute the hypothetical came to his mind, he began to think. All the places Mr. Williams had shown him in his albums, places of unimaginable beauty, truly existed and were out there waiting for him to see. But how could he? Stormboy belonged here in Westside, and that was that. Freight Train would've never had these thoughts

Everything for them.

That settled it. It was no wonder he had repeated the motto so often. Freight Train was the wisest man he'd ever known; he had to have come across similar situations to his. At the end of it all, the motto held true. He stood by that— he had to. Although the thought had been nice, if only for a moment.

"Hey, Sammy!" A familiar voice called from behind him. It was Darius being swallowed by an enormous amount of grocery bags. He waved him down, his arms flexed from the weight of milk, sodas, and other food products. "You think you can give them a hand?"

Darius threw his head back, gesturing to his two little girls. His oldest was clutching a whole frozen chicken in one hand and a bag of snacks in the other, but it was the younger one he was referring to. The poor thing had a bag she had grown tired of lifting and instead dragged it across the pavement. The plastic bag was shredded against the clanging canned goods inside. When Sam finally took it from her, the bag was barely intact. Sam had helped relieve some of Darius's weight as well.

"I owe you one."

It was the least he could do. Darius and his girls had been his neighbors for as long as he lived there. His late hours as Stormboy couldn't be easy for him. He had tried his best to be as quiet as possible coming home, but sometimes, after all his crusading, his body would stumble home noisily. Besides— *everything for them.* He wondered if there was anything else he could do, outside of Stormboy, to help people.

"Thanks, pal. You're my hero."

"Thank you, Mr. Sam," the two girls said in unison. Samual and Darius walked side by side while the two girls skipped out in front of them.

"So how did things go with that crazy woman?"

Samual blushed.

"She's fine. I helped her out a while back, and she was just returning the favor."

Darius's eyebrows attempted to leap off his face as a crazy grin manifested.

"You dog!" Darius screeched; Samual was left confused. "She's a good-looking girl. Nice job! I always knew you had it in you!"

Sam's face flushed as he now realized what Darius was talking about.

"It's not like that! She just helped with some stuff around

the house, that's all!" Darius could not contain his laughter.

"She wears one of those cute little maid skirts while she does it, too, I bet!"

Although the thought of Samantha wearing a maid uniform intrigued him, Sam shook his head furiously.

"But do you like her?"

Darius's words lingered, and the whole world stopped.

Do I?

"She's just a girl," he said with as much assuredness as he could muster. Admittedly, it wasn't much.

"All right, I hear ya!" The smile didn't leave his face, and Sam could have sworn he heard a little snicker from the two little girls up ahead.

"So, how have you been?" Darius changed the subject. "You seem tired."

He was more referring to the condition of his face; Sam appreciated his discreetness about the whole thing. "It ain't any of my business, but try not to look like that around my girls."

His girls were always the first and last thing on his mind. Samual respected that about him. They may not have talked too often to each other, but he was the closest thing Sam had to a friend. Throughout the years, he would watch Sam come home late at night beat up. He questioned it at first, wondering if he belonged to a gang or something. Fitting, of course— he wanted to keep his girls as far away from that as possible. The more they spent time together, though, the more he realized that whatever was going on was none of his business. He had eventually stopped asking about it, but still shook his head whenever he saw him.

"Work has been taking a lot out of me recently."

"Late hours?"

Sam simply nodded.

"I don't know what you got going on, but promise me you will take some time out to relax and heal. You are only human, Sam."

If only he knew how "human" he really was. That if he wasn't eternally mindful, he could nuke an entire block in an instant. It was bad enough for Samantha to know who he was, and as much as he wanted to tell Darius the truth and put his mind at some kind of ease, Mr. Kain's code always persisted.

"I'll try." It was a lie. A necessary one, but a lie, nonetheless.

When they finally arrived at their apartment complex, the girls ran out in front of them up the stairs. Darius shouted after them to be careful, but the two were already safely up the stairs.

"You got your hands full with those two," Sam chuckled.

"Yeah, I worry, but they are good kids. They can take care of themselves."

"They have a good dad."

"Eh, maybe that, too." The two exchanged handshakes, before going their separate ways.

"Bye, Mr. Sam." The three of them disappeared into their home, leaving Sam alone. Today was strange. He had cleaned his home with Samantha, walked her most of the way home, and then hung out with his neighbor.

Did Freight Train have days like this? Days where he was just Mr. Kain and nothing else?

Even the thought made him shutter, it was like he was violating some sort of unspoken rule living this way and enjoying it. Was it impossible to live a normal life while also being Stormboy?

Everything for them.

Everything else was a distraction. This is the code. He did a poor job of convincing himself.

CHAPTER 5

FIVE YEARS AGO

Stormboy had been at his post where Freight Train had told him to be for over an hour. Stormboy sat there waiting, anxiously, before suddenly he appeared, leaping from the ground floor to the roof to join him.

"Where have you been?" Stormboy asked, concerned. He was typically so prompt, but the more he thought about it the more he knew Freight Train wasn't going to explain himself. He never did.

"I apologize, Stormboy. I had business." He had a smile that plastered his face, but it didn't fool him! His smile was usually so reassuring, one that said that he was here to comfort and protect, but this smile was different. He hadn't quite put his finger on it, but something had changed in Freight Train. He was always off on "business" and never let Stormboy in on the secret. It was beginning to affect their work.

"Of course. Business," Stormboy repeated.

"Come on! Everything is fine. I'm here."

It did little to reassure him, but he had to listen to his teacher.

"Besides, it gives you a chance to learn. I'm not always going to be here, ya know?" Freight Train gave him a slight pat on the back. Stormboy wasn't buying it— something was up, and Freight Train was sidestepping the question. It was best not to push it any further, though. They had a job to do.

"Well, now that you are here, we can start, right?"

"Right!" Freight Train reiterated, and the two were off. They had patrol routes every night that Stormboy had to memorize. Every day, they ran a new route, one of eight, and stopped any sort of crime they had spotted along the way. Stormboy had been doing this for about three years now and was finally getting to the point where he was getting used to jumping the rooftops and scaling the buildings to navigate the city efficiently. However, he was nothing compared to Freight Train. His raw strength allowed him feats Stormboy could only dream of. His mentor had to intentionally slow down to allow him to keep up.

They reached their first rest stop on this particular route. There was a condemned building set for demolition, but the city was too poor to get anyone to knock it down, so there it stood for the past three years, empty and abandoned. It made for a good place to recoup.

"You're moving quite well today, Stormboy. You are getting a lot stronger!" Freight Train said.

It felt good to hear, but it didn't feel warranted. He was being overly nice. There was no way he could ever keep up, but instead of starting the argument, he just took the backhanded compliment in stride.

"Thank you, sir."

"Sir?" Freight Train laughed. "Since when did you start calling me 'sir'?"

"Since when do you show up late for patrols?" He was so tired of trying to keep up with him his internal censors had completely shut down. The words flowed right out of him without thinking, quick and sharp, like a bolt of lightning.

"Hey, that's not fair! You got to cut this old man some slack now and then."

Slack?

Stormboy remembered the early days of his training. How hard he had pushed him to be better. He didn't think slack was in Freight Train's vocabulary.

Where was the slack in the rubber room?

That damn rubber room! It had been his home for two years. Mr. Kain had instructed him to keep his power completely contained and when he could prove he could completely control his power, he could leave. Now and then he would come and share a meal with Sam in the room. He would do everything he could to keep his power contained, but especially in those early days, it just wasn't possible. His powers would flare, and Freight Train would respond with a punch to the gut.

"Breathe," his mentor would mutter as he attempted to quiet the storm.

"Breathe!" he repeated before striking him again. Sam recounted all the times he'd writhe and cry on the floor, trying to catch his breath. Sam's power would lash out in his defense, sometimes so violently it would send Freight Train clear across the room. But still, he persisted, and despite all the pain and suffering, it worked. Freight Train had sacrificed himself being in that room with him for those two years. The number of times he left the rubber room twitching from the amount of voltage Sam had pumped into him, and still, he cared enough to come back the next day. He had control over his abilities because of how hard Freight Train had been on him. He still wasn't perfect, but he was a far cry from sneaking out for nightly "discharges."

"Sure, slack." Stormboy stood and dusted himself off. "Ready when you are, or does the old man need more time to rest?"

Freight Train let out a deep-bellied laugh.

"The mighty Stormboy likes to joke!" He sprang to his feet so quickly that when his feet hit the floor, he almost took the whole building with him. "Lead the way, hero!"

The night went on like always. Most people saw the two of them and suddenly had second thoughts about any petty crimes they were planning. No one's wallet was worth the combined might of Freight Train and Stormboy. Sam was getting used to this lifestyle. The frightened boy in the rubber room had evolved into a full-fledged hero! Well, a full-fledged sidekick, at least. What was once tiring or frightening now felt routine. He had leaped to people in need without a second thought. When the two of them spotted two rival gangs caught up in a turf war, he leaped in with his mentor and quickly dispatched the situation before it got out of hand. He was saving lives, as his powers had always been meant to do.

"Let's stop here a moment." Freight Train spoke, and Sam obeyed. They were close to finishing up their night; he wondered why he would take the time to stop now. "Samual. I think you are ready."

"Sir, shouldn't you be calling me Stormboy?"

"You're right." He gave Sam a playful nudge on his shoulder. What was up with him today? He seemed off somehow.

"You have shown tremendous promise these past few months. I believe you are ready to patrol on your own."

The world stopped.

"Are you sure?" Sam questioned.

He couldn't be serious.

"I am," Freight Train responded.

I can't do that!

"I don't know if I can."

"You can!" His heavy hand clasped against Stormboy's shoulder. "Stormboy. You knew this time would eventually come. There are times when I'm going to have to be other places ..."

"On business?" Stormboy interrupted. Freight Train could only smile.

"Maybe. But regardless, I have full faith in you. I wouldn't be telling you this otherwise."

"But what if I hurt someone? I could forget a route and

get caught off guard. I'm only this good because you are here with me!"

"Breathe!" His voice boomed. Stormboy flinched at the words. Thoughts of the rubber room came to him. How he could so easily lose control. "Do you trust me?"

Samual stared at his hands unsurely. But if not him, who else could he trust? If Freight Train said he could do it, then he must be able to. So, he nodded.

"It's time to have faith in yourself. You must start seeing yourself the way I see you and I promise in time, they'll see, too."

They adjusted their focus to the city.

"This is the beginning of your journey. It's time for you to rise, Stormboy. To become the hero of Westside I always knew you could be."

The sun peaked above the horizon, and Stormboy caught a hint of his mentor's expression.

This had always been the endgame. What I've been working toward.

An uncomfortable feeling wouldn't leave his stomach, and as much as he tried to, Stormboy found it hard to breathe. He finally managed to speak.

"I'm ready."

CHAPTER 6

WESTSIDE WOK

Samual awoke on the couch in a stupor. He expected to open his eyes, don his uniform, and make his way to patrol the city, but the sun shining took him off guard. His apartment, still clean from his last encounter with Samantha, felt foreign to him. The clock read 6:00 pm, still earlier than he had been used to. She messed him up! He would typically be asleep the entire day so that he could be ready for his night's work.

It's fine . . . Everything is fine!

He gathered his things and began to head toward his front door. He turned to look at his place. Nothing felt right anymore.

What did she do to me?

It was a bit of a relief. Something he hadn't expected. His life felt different in a way, but what it was he couldn't be sure. What an odd feeling.

On the ground by the door was a collection of letters dropped from the mail carrier. Sam skimmed through it, only looking for one thing in particular. A statement from the bank. Mr. Kain had kept a large sum of money set aside for him that he monitored extremely closely. No penny went unaccounted for in his monthly spending, another habit picked up from his old mentor. Sam figured that's probably how Mr. Kain obtained the vast wealth to begin with. He could never repay him for all that he had given him. Maybe Stormboy could though.

Sam's stomach growled ferociously. He gathered his things and just as he opened his front door, he was stopped by the sudden appearance of his muse who started all this. Her face was shocked at Samual's sudden appearance.

"It's like you felt me coming." She gave a wry, nervous smile.

"Why are you here?" he said. "The job is done. The place is clean—we're even."

"Well, maybe there was something else I could do. Besides, I feel a bit bad for the way I ditched you last time," she replied. "I still sort of owe you."

"You don't owe me anything."

"I owe you my life."

She was relentless. No matter what Sam said after this point was useless.

"It's my job!" Sam tried to push past her. There was no use in arguing any further. Trying his best to ignore her, he made his way down the stairs.

"Where are you going?" she said insistently as she followed close behind.

"I have nothing for you today." Walking down the stairs, he stopped momentarily and looked back at her. His eyes caught hers. She had curled her hair now. He didn't think it possible for her to look more stunning than before, but she managed somehow. Sam couldn't help but notice a tiny golden locket around her neck that she grabbed nervously. It had a tiny engraving he couldn't quite make out. She bit her bottom lip; she had this look of sadness about her that Sam couldn't look past. He let out a long sigh. "I'm going to get something to eat."

"Excellent, I'll join you!"

Sam navigated his mind to search for any good collection

of words he could string together to make it so that didn't happen.

"I know a great sushi place. Come on!" She hopped down the steps and was now somehow leading the way. The words wouldn't reach him and before he realized it, he was on his way to dinner with her.

Do I even like Sushi?

Sam went back in his mind to the last time he shared a meal with someone. Thoughts of the rubber room came to him, but other than the old days with Mr. Kain, there was nothing. This kind of luxury was something he couldn't wrap his head around. It made him feel like a toddler taking his first steps into the world. He was nervous, but kept pace with Samantha.

The streets were filled with people. Families gathered, laughing and joking; some locals were throwing dice on their stoops, cussing to each other while local musicians lined the streets, blurting renditions of old classics, which had the crowd dancing and clapping along.

"This city is something, isn't it?" Samantha tried to make herself heard over all the noise. She was walking and clapping along, not noticing Sam had fallen behind. He tried to politely squeeze his way through, gently apologizing as Samantha got further and further away from him. She was right at home here. She was dancing effortlessly through the crowd, swinging and spinning. They finally made it to a small clearing. Samantha had almost pirouetted out of the crowd as Samual came stumbling behind her.

"It's something all right." Samual fixed himself as the strenuous journey had thrown him more than he expected.

"Are you OK?" She leaned in toward him.

"I'm fine," he replied. "Just hungry."

She reached over and took his hand. It should've been nothing—a simple gesture. Sam's heart had stopped.

"Don't worry, we're almost there." Her smile was comforting, and he gave in as she pulled him down a few more blocks.

"Westside Wok?"

They both stopped in front of a tiny establishment in the basement of some grocery store in the middle of 42nd Street. No wonder Samual had never heard of it. The sign denoting its existence was a whiteboard placed on an easel with a crude arrow pointing downward. The street was already dominated by the lights of the fashion boutiques 42nd Street was known for. It was an odd place for a restaurant, to say the least. Samual raised an eyebrow toward Samantha, but she was already halfway down the stairs.

"Hurry up!" She waved her hand and pointed down to the cellar. "You were the one who said you were hungry!"

He must've passed this place dozens of times; how had he never seen it before? They opened the door and were greeted by the host, who showed them to their seat. An awkward silence persisted as Samual tried to make sense of the menu in front of him. His eyes kept leaping up and down between her and the menu, struggling to figure out the proper etiquette in such a situation. It was as if the entire restaurant was watching and judging him.

"What was he doing here? Why does he look so odd?" The words in his head kept pelting him as if they were being screamed in his ears by every patron there. He sank lower and lower into his chair.

"So." Samantha's soft voice pierced through the storm in his mind. "What do you think?"

"I don't know what I'm doing here. I feel odd." His face was barely visible over his menu, but Samantha just laughed, and Sam blushed.

"Don't worry, I can order for you."

It was kind of her but not really what he meant when he said he didn't know what he was doing. The waiter came around, and Samantha slapped together a series of words that he could only assume would result in food in front of him. The waiter left as quickly as he came, and the two were stuck with each other. Samual's eyes wandered all over the restaurant trying to avoid Samantha, who fixated on him.

"You don't get out too often, do you?" Samantha asked.

Samual was somewhere else; more than anything, he wanted to get out of there and head home. Every situation ran through his head, and they all ended with him either embarrassed or hurt. His hands clenched so tightly, they began to sweat.

"Hey, it's OK." Her words broke through to him again. Sam did what he could to nudge himself back up in his chair. He hadn't realized how low he sank and how awkward he must've seemed.

"No . . ." He paused for just a second longer than what would've been normal. "I don't get out often."

Samantha seemed surprised. Just that one sentence felt like a marathon.

Why do I feel so exhausted?

"You don't have any friends or anything?"

"My line of work doesn't leave room for friends."

"Why not?"

Here we go again!

Samual should've expected this.

"Too dangerous. People get close, they realize what you are, and they can't handle it. Better off to be on your own. Besides, everything for them."

It had always been like this.

Connections are cancer.

Mr. Kain's words came to him. It made sense, though. Why endanger anyone unnecessarily? Samual turned his head to a painting of a mountain pinned to the wall. It was a magnificent mural of a snowcapped peak with the sun shining down brilliantly in the back. If he squinted hard enough, it was almost as if someone was nearing the peak. On the bottom in bold red letters, it said, "Triumph."

"But what about you?" Samantha asked.

"What do you mean?" Samual snapped back at her, confused.

"Well, you push everyone out of your life and keep them away from you. How do you feel about it?"

Samual paused for a second. The thought never occurred to him before. At the end of the day, what did it matter?

The waiter came through and placed two plates in front of them. Samantha squealed and applauded with excitement before snapping her chopsticks open. Samual peered down at his plate. It was certainly colorful. He took the first roll in his fingers and plopped it into his mouth. He was surprised. This neatly packed roll burst into flavors in his mouth, many of which he didn't recognize.

I do like sushi!

A smile grew on his face, and he went to grab another. Seconds before it reached his mouth, he was interrupted.

"How about using a fork at least." Samantha looked at him strangely. They stared at each other for a moment, and Samual plopped another roll into his mouth. Samantha cocked her head. Finally, he was the one who caught her off guard!

"OK. Fine!" As if not to be beaten, Samantha audibly slammed her sticks on the table and picked up her sushi and tossed it to the back of her throat. Her mouth curled into a smile, distorted only by her chewing. The two traded back and forth, sometimes not even waiting to swallow the previous roll before shoving another into their face. Plop, plop, plop, plop, plop!

"How are we doing?" The waiter was making his rounds. Samantha turned violently.

"Another boat for the table, please!"

The dinner had become a competition. Each one fighting to throw another roll back to not show weakness to the other. Samual didn't know how the sushi, being so tiny, had managed to take up so much room in his stomach, but he refused to quit.

"Anything else?" The waiter came back around. The two of them didn't break eye contact. Samual was visibly breathing while Samantha held her stomach in silent agony. Their eyes, however, remained thin with intensity. "Because we've been closed for twenty minutes."

The two of them looked up from each other to see that the restaurant was completely deserted, save for the employees who were waiting for them to get up so they could go home. How long had it been? Samual wondered.

"Oh my God!" Samantha threw her hands over her mouth. The waiter lurched forward in case she was preparing to spew her dinner over the table.

"Yes, we are good. I am so sorry!" Samual bowed his head in shame. The waiter left, clearly aggravated. They both held their breath in anticipation, and as soon as he left earshot, as if they were following similar cues, gave in to their laughter. It was an uncontrollable fit that Samual hadn't felt in such a long time.

The streets were a bit calmer now. More to what Samual was accustomed to. They walked shoulder to shoulder down the streets of Westside. It had been some time now, and Samual realized they had not spoken a word to each other since they left the restaurant. He looked at her, and he could tell she felt uncomfortable. He had hoped it was due to the hoard of food they had just eaten and not the silence between them. Everything in him wanted to say something, but everything that came to him came with a caveat.

That's dumb. That would only make her mad! Connections are cancer. Shake it off, Sammy!

"So, I'm pretty sure I won, right?" she said.

Samual was secretly waiting for her to break the silence. It was like a superpower she had; she always knew exactly what to say at any given moment.

"What do you mean?"

"Please! Stop acting like you didn't know what was going on!"

"All right, fine!" Samual laughed. "But you definitely didn't win."

"What are you talking about? I kept up with you the entire time. Tit for tat! I didn't skip a beat! I'm quite proud of myself."

"Yeah, but I ate that one in the beginning before we even started going at it. Besides, I also snuck in a few while you were holding your stomach!"

"Bullshit!"

"I couldn't wait for you. You're a slow eater!"

"You are so full of it!" Samantha finally said, crossing her arms. Samual just stared at her, smiling.

"So, is it OK for us to be friends like this?" She retreated into herself as she waited for his response. He knew what he wanted to say, but no matter how hard he tried, the only words that came out of his mouth were . . .

"I don't know."

An unsettling silence took them, and Samantha broke away from him to walk a few paces ahead.

"So, Freight Train . . . he raised you, right?"

"Most foster families didn't know how to handle a lightning child. He accepted the challenge. So, yeah."

"And how was that?" she asked.

"He was a good mentor. Taught me everything I needed to know about being a man and being a hero."

"Like screw everyone and be alone forever?"

"Mr. Kain cared about me! If you haven't noticed, I'm not a normal guy! He did what he had to protect me."

"Protect you from what?"

"From everyone!"

This is what he was used to. The arguing, the shame.

Why is it so hard to look at her?

"Do you feel protected?"

"Of course I do! Look at me. I'm safe. Everyone is safe, right?"

"OK, but are you happy?"

It didn't matter how tall she actually was. She was looking down at him now.

"Of course," Sam said. "I'm a superhero. The ultimate force for good in this city. People hear the name Stormboy, and they feel safe. Protected."

"That's not what I asked, though."

Samual chuckled at her words, which only made her mad.

"What's so funny?" Samantha stomped furiously.

"You have this way about you. My mind races around you, so I try to prepare for anything you might say. But I'm wrong every time."

Samantha didn't even hesitate to respond.

"It's because I care about you, Sam. But you seem to think that that doesn't matter."

Connection is cancer.

Everything for them!

Everything for them?

"But I'm Stormboy." His voice cracked as he spoke.

"You know, I really am starting to think you aren't." They had been frozen on the sidewalk for some time, and she finally made her way toward him. "I've seen Stormboy on the news. Hell, Stormboy saved me once."

"So, if I'm not Stormboy, then who am I?"

Samantha smiled. "You are Sam. A sweet, if a little disorganized, bachelor in an apartment in the slums of Westside. He may be a little unsure of himself and lets his mind get in the way of things he wants to do, but he tries to be kind to those around him. Including allowing strangers to go out on dinner dates with him."

Samual couldn't help but blush.

"And why do you think I did that?" Samual asked.

"Because you are too sweet for your own good." Samantha giggled. "But that's what I like about you. You are unconditionally kind."

A warmness washed over him.

"Despite everything you might be feeling, you still do what's best for others. It makes for a great hero, but not much else."

She placed a hand on his cheek.

"Maybe," he whispered. She pulled away.

"Come on." The two of them continued down the street, once again walking together. Before they knew it, they were outside Samual's apartment.

"Thank you for spending time with me," Samual said. It made him feel foolish.

"Sam, I think you've done enough, don't you?" Samual's heart fluttered. "I really enjoyed myself tonight, but if I never came back, how would you feel?"

Samual couldn't bring himself to respond. Too many variables and situations came to his mind. The field he understood, the mind of a criminal he could comprehend—why not his own? He wanted to avoid the question.

"Do you need me to walk you home?" He was conflicted about which answer he was looking for. On the one hand, he wanted to stay with her, on the other hand, the difficulty of the conversation weighed on him.

Everything for them! No, stop it!

Samantha shook her head.

"I don't think I need Stormboy tonight." They both waited at his door.

"Have a good night, Sam," he said to her, shyly.

"Are you going out tonight?" She responded, and Samual nodded. She approached him and gave him a tight hug. "Please be safe."

He felt her more than her words. She was so soft. He didn't want this moment to end. Just being held by someone who cared. He was flushed with heat and his heartbeat was ferocious. He swallowed persistently to keep it down.

"Of course. I'm Stormboy." She broke the embrace and shook her head.

"Yeah, you are." She turned to leave him. Samual wanted to tell her everything she wanted to hear, anything that would convince her to stay. The disappointment on both their faces wasn't lost on him.

CHAPTER 7

PHANTOM

Stormboy loved the rooftops. Everything was calm here. No one challenged him. With a slow exhale, he let his power surge. The electricity jumped from his body, across the power lines, along the streets and electrical boxes of the neighboring apartment buildings. He felt alive! His mind wandered to Samantha in this moment of freedom. It had been nearly a week since he'd seen her, and her words still haunted him. Streams of lightning crossed his vision as he gazed out onto the city. Everything was so calm—why wasn't he? Any sort of movement in the city below made him jump.

Someone has to be committing a crime somewhere!

His eyes darted in every direction in a desperate attempt at something, anything that would allow him to escape his head.

What if she never comes back? Why do you care so much?

Every question was a punch in the gut.

"You seem distracted, Stormboy." A familiar voice pierced the storm, and his lightning ceased. He turned to see the bulky frame of his former mentor. His spandex was loud and bombastic, which was fitting if you knew the man behind the mask.

How?

Freight Train made his way to the edge of the building and gazed out toward the city with dominance. It was always impressive to see his confidence. It was as if his shadow had eclipsed the entire city; its essence absorbed into him. He finally turned to face Stormboy. His stature even obscured the full moon from view. He felt so small.

"Is there something you want to tell me?" Freight Train placed his hands on his hips, the hero of Westside in full view, but to Stormboy, it was a concerned parent ready to scold. He turned back to the city.

"I'm fine," he lied. "I'm fully focused."

Freight Train's laugh hit like a sonic boom. "Talk to me, boy. What's on your mind? You can't save anyone in your condition."

How could Sam possibly tell him? How could he look him in the eye, the man who raised him, made him who he was today, and tell him he was questioning the life he made for him?

"Were you happy being Freight Train?"

"I was the greatest hero this city has ever seen! Without me, this place would have imploded on itself. I took on so many crime bosses and drug dealers, that people are now able to walk these streets and not have to worry about getting caught up in something dangerous."

"I know, I know. I'm not questioning that. But were YOU happy? Was there any room for you in all of that?"

"What does that matter?"

"They didn't hate you like they do me! Most people think I'm doing more harm than good."

Freight Train stepped closer to Stormboy. So close, he had to step back or get thrown down.

"Have you forgotten everything I've taught you? What's our mantra—the very first rule?"

"Everything for . . ." Stormboy exhaled it before being

interrupted by the thunderous bass of Freight Train's voice.

"EVERYTHING FOR THEM!"

Stormboy cowered. He refused to keep eye contact but still felt his shadow lingering over him. The mantra kept repeating over and over, echoing in his head until it pervaded everything he was. It was overwhelming; he wanted to shove his hands into his skull. But somehow, deep inside, he found strength. He remembered her words.

"But what about me?" Her words pierced the mantra he had kept at the center of his reality for so long. It was such a simple thing he couldn't understand why it never came to him before.

"What?" Freight Train retorted; he was growing smaller now.

"You raised me and gave me so much guidance, and I can never repay you for that. But 'Everything for them' leaves nothing for me!"

A scream broke the silence of the city, and before his mind could figure out something more to say, his body reacted. Everything was a blur. His body was acting on pure instinct. Stormboy pursued the scream with furious passion. Across the rooftops and up and down alleys until he reached the scene.

"Oh shit—Stormboy!" The man quickly grabbed his hostage and unsheathed a switchblade. "Don't take another step, hero!"

Stormboy took a second and examined the situation. A man on the ground bleeding, clutching his nose.

Boyfriend, maybe? Tried defending the hostage?

The hostage's clothes were slightly tattered, and her dress sleeve was pulled halfway down her arm. He made it just in time.

"Take it easy. Let's not let this get out of hand."

The woman was strong. Tears were streaming down her face, but she wouldn't scream. The perp knew he was losing control of the situation. He was frantically trying to walk backward and drag the girl with him.

"Just walk away man, this has nothing to do with you!"

"I just don't want to see anyone get hurt." Stormboy knew if he let his powers loose, he might accidentally hurt the girl, too. "Just let her go and get out of here, and we can all just forget this happened."

Stormboy was talking out of his ass, but he had to rein in the situation. He stepped over to the downed boyfriend.

"Hey, what are you doing?" the perp said, digging the knife closer to the girl's throat. Samual placed both his hands up in a defensive posture.

"I just want to see if he's OK."

"You need to get out of here Stormboy. That asshole had it coming!"

"And her?"

"Wrong place, wrong time." The girl was now on her tip-toes, struggling to keep the blade from slitting her neck.

"This isn't worth it; just let the girl go, and we can talk this out."

"Don't bullshit me, Stormboy! I'm not an idiot. Walk away or else she dies!" The girl simply closed her eyes tighter. Stormboy looked at the boyfriend. He was so scared he wouldn't even look up. Stormboy had considered everything and knew he had only one option. He began to back away.

"That's it . . . just walk away!" Stormboy eventually turned his back on the three of them.

"No, Stormboy, please." It was the first time the woman had spoken. Stormboy heard her plea, but kept walking. The perp spat in his direction. His confidence in himself was growing. He laid off the woman and began to curse at Stormboy waving his knife in the air.

"Who knew the 'Hero of Westside' was such a little bitch!" His confidence inflated to such a point that he had now been swinging the woman by her hair in one hand and flashing obscene gestures with the other. Stormboy just continued walking away, ignoring his mockery while secretly allowing his power to flourish into his index finger. The perp turned as if to address Westside itself. "Run away with your tail between your legs! The whole city is going to know that Stormboy was beaten by—"

Stormboy whisked around suddenly, and lightning flashed from his finger straight through the shoulder of the perp. The shot took him straight off his feet as the girl collapsed to her knees.

Thank God!

Stormboy approached the criminal and checked for a pulse before checking on the woman.

"Are you OK?"

Her tears were relentless; her legs gave out, and she fell into Stormboy's arms. She was holding him so tight he could feel each nail digging into his skin. But she was safe. He guided her to her boyfriend, who he had helped to his feet.

"You two should get of here. I'll stay here and make sure this guy gets what he deserves." The woman let out a yelp, and the boyfriend took measures to protect her.

"Look out!" the boyfriend yelled. Stormboy swung around as fast as he could. The switchblade met his cheek, and he was sliced from the corner of his eye down to the lip.

I thought I had him!

Stormboy's power began to surge violently.

"Oh, crap!" The perp tucked the blade away and made his escape down the dark alley.

Relax Sam! Just breathe!

Stormboy took a few seconds to himself to allow the electricity to subside.

Not now.

"Oh my God, are you OK?" The woman asked.

Sloppy!

"I'm fine. You two should get home though in case he tries to come back." The two of them looked grateful and left with urgency. Which just left Stormboy. The ambiance of the city drowned away, and he was left with the sound of his own breathing. He gently dabbed the side of his face, checking for the severity of the wound.

Again! I let my guard down again! On top of that I almost lost control. Stupid!

"How could you let that punk sneak up on you?" The familiar voice from earlier emerged from the shadows of the alley. Freight Train's image melded out of the shadow to look down on the new scar he had on his face. "You are better than this!"

"Shut up! I don't have to listen to you anymore." His mentor wasn't making this any easier on him.

"Please, you've been listening to me this whole time." No matter how hard Stormboy tried to pull away, the shadow followed. "You've never stopped listening to me, and you never will. I don't even think you know how."

"Shut up!" Sam shouted in the now empty alley. His head began to pound, but he wasn't sure if it was due to the wound or due to something else. Despite all his confusion, there was one thing he knew for certain he needed to do. There was a part of town he had been avoiding for some time now, but tonight was the night he knew he had to return to it.

There were a few lights still on, just enough for the night security to make their rounds, and the few lights that illuminated the stone slab out front that read "Westside Cemetery." He had always thought of coming here more often, but never did. Maybe he was just afraid to see him again, to reaffirm what he already knew about his mentor. He wasn't sure of the reason, but tonight he had to see him again. The lawn was littered with tiny lights that illuminated the walkways. Stormboy had to be careful of course, he had to not only remain in the shadows, but he'd try his best to not desecrate any burial site on the way to his destination. He thought he might have trouble finding it after all this time, but before he knew it, he was there. "KAIN." The mausoleum read in great bold letters. How Mr. Kain was able to afford this after he had died, Sam never knew, but it was all he had left physically to hold on to him. His mentor. His father.

"What are you doing here?" A bright light shone directly on his face.

I guess I wasn't as quiet as I thought.

"Hey, Ron." Thank God he recognized the voice. Ron was the night watchman at the cemetery. He could barely keep his back straight, much less do anything to any trespasser, but he was an old hard-ass that didn't take any nonsense from anyone. He held the keys to the mausoleum; he knew what was inside, or rather, who. He was a good friend, one who could keep secrets.

"Damn, boy! You scared the hell out of me. Never seen you come out here in a while. Everything OK?" Ron looked concerned. "What happened to your face?"

"It's fine. You think I could see him?"

"I don't see why not. Try not to make it a habit of coming at this time. You're gonna put me in the ground with all of them other folk." Ron reached for one specific key and tossed it to Stormboy. "Just come find me when you're done. I'll be around."

"Thanks, Ron." Stormboy turned and unlocked the door.

"Here, take this." Ron pulled out a rag and dampened it with some water. "It's something for now."

Stormboy smiled and placed it on his cheek before entering the tomb.

This place always amazed him. It almost seemed as if it were bigger on the inside than it was on the outside. It was mostly due to the large statue perched on the back wall. Encased in stone was Freight Train himself, hands on his hips with that trademark smile, looking down on all those who entered. His smile always managed to bring a calmness to people, but not Sam. At the foot of the statue lay his coffin with a stone plaque reading:

Here Lies Edward Kain
Freight Train
Hero

Hero. He removed his mask and hood and placed his right hand on the coffin.

"Mr. Kain. What am I doing?" A gust of air whipped through the carved vents; the whistle it caused echoed through the chamber.

"You're doing what you've always done." Freight Train appeared behind him as if from nowhere. "You're kicking ass and saving lives."

"Then why do I feel this way?" Samual's eyes were kept fixed on the coffin. "You've taught me so much, but I'm not prepared for this. I wasn't ready to be left alone."

It seemed his mentor had laughed, but it was masked by another gust of wind that whisked through.

"You're as dramatic as ever," Freight Train said as he loomed over Sam. "Nothing has changed; you're doing great. The city is safe. What more do you need?"

He was right. He had a responsibility to the city. Nothing else should matter.

"Tell me something, Sammy."

Sam had closed his eyes briefly before turning to meet his gaze. Six foot six inches and 280 pounds of pure power.

"When you saved that couple tonight, how did you feel?"

Samual thought about it. He went back to that moment in the alley earlier in the evening.

"That's not the point."

"That's exactly the point!" his voice boomed. Sam flinched. "You say you don't know, but you know exactly what you're doing. It doesn't matter if what you're doing is making you happy or not, you have a responsibility to those people, and you can't seem to admit to yourself that you might be born to do it!" Sam tried to match his gaze, but the thunderous bass in Freight Train's voice pushed his face toward the ground. Sam's eyes eventually met his feet and again he felt defeated.

A scared child—again!

There was a long silence only broken by Sam's sobbing. He eventually pulled his head up and Freight Train was nowhere to be seen. He turned again to the statue; it simply smiled back.

CHAPTER 8

MY FAVORITE SPOT

Samual had half hoped that his neighbors would be up in arms. He had been hoping for some unsuspecting visitor to be causing a disturbance at his door, but still nothing. Samual made his way to his feet. His apartment was a mess, but he couldn't help but crack a smile. The exasperated look of Samantha gazing at his apartment left him jubilant. With all his late hours and early mornings, he had been too exhausted to maintain any semblance of organization or cleanliness in his home. What was the point? Who knows, maybe she had a sixth sense for this stuff, and she would come knowing it was time to help him.

Is that all she is to you? A maid?

The jubilance quickly turned to shame. He left his home and gazed out at the city. Westside was his to roam, but nowhere was interesting enough to go. Sam had no place to be. Everything felt futile. He had thought about turning around and going back inside, but that somehow felt worse. He forced his feet forward and down his stairs with no destination in mind.

The streets were alive as ever. Shopkeepers were shouting their sales to pedestrians, and kids were playing games impatiently as they made their way to the park. Sam couldn't help but smile. This was his city. The city Freight Train had entrusted to him. He spent the five years protecting these streets alone, and maybe this was the reward. Maybe this was enough.

He passed the shopping district and continued meandering until he reached the hospital. So many people had ended up here at Westside General because of him. Well, him and his "talent." They had hurt so many people that Sam tended to stay away from this place. So much guilt. The building stood three stories tall.

I wonder how much of this place I've filled up?

His mind wandered to the many crimes he'd stopped and the countless people he had hurt in the process. Guilty or otherwise. Was this also a part of it? If he hadn't been here and done all that he'd done, hurt all those people? Is this the legacy he wanted to leave behind for himself? The ward of Freight Train, best known for filling the emergency ward!

Everything for them. But they still deserve better.

A few hospital employees walked in his direction. As they approached, Sam snapped back to reality. He realized he had been staring at the building for an unusually long time and thought he should probably go before questions began to arise.

"So, you're stalking me now?"

"No, no, I'm sorry. I was . . ."

Not the question I was expecting! Wait. That could only mean . . .

Sam readjusted his focus to realize that one of those nurses was Samantha. Her hair was knotted in an unkempt bun. She was probably exhausted, but she looked as magnificent as ever. She wore a teal uniform, much like her other coworkers, that laid loose on her torso. Her hips jutted outward as she stared at Sam in disbelief.

"I honestly didn't know you worked here," Samual said, embarrassed.

"Yup, that's what a stalker would say," one of the other nurses said before the third joined her in a giggle. Sam swallowed the lump in his throat. Samantha waved good-bye to her friends, reassuring them that she would be safe.

"So, what are you doing here?" Samantha said. Her voice was so soothing, probably because she was so exhausted. She didn't have the energy to be mad at him.

"I have no idea." Sam looked away and shoved his hands firmly into his pockets. The silence between them was weighing them down.

"You going to tell me what happened to your face?" She gestured to his cheek. The scar from the previous night was still clearly visible.

"Occupational hazard," Sam responded. Samantha rolled her eyes.

"You didn't even clean it properly. It looks bad."

"It's fine."

"Unacceptable! Come with me!" Samantha grabbed his hand so quickly he could barely react and led him on a journey, as she tends to do. First to a convenience store where they got the necessary first aid supplies, then to a quiet spot where she could treat him.

"So are you going to tell me what happened?" Finding a spot in Westside where there weren't constant people around was nearly impossible, but they found a bench where they would at least be ignored. People tended to mind their own business around here, especially when it came to someone with a giant gash across his face. Sam obeyed her as she shoved and maneuvered him to sit down. She leaned in, her mouth slightly agape in deep concentration, and dabbed the wound with a cotton swab.

"I told you, work stuff." Her face had been so close to his, he began to blush.

"Indulge me. I love asking my patients about their injuries. They are usually very eager to share." Sam looked at her as there was nowhere else to look. Her brown eyes shone in the sunlight like amber jewels. He couldn't take his eyes off her. Well even if he wanted to, he couldn't.

I can see why! Who wouldn't want to talk to an angel like her?

"Why didn't you tell me you were a nurse?"

"Why are you avoiding my question?" She pressed on a sensitive spot with her swab, and Sam retreated in pain. "Oh please, hero!"

There's the Samantha he'd grown to love.

"It was a robbery," Samual began to explain. "Guy had a couple at knifepoint. Lost focus for a second and got cut. No big deal."

"Yeah . . . no big deal." Samantha pulled back her cotton swab now thoroughly soaked in Sam's blood.

"Why is me being Stormboy such an issue to you?"

She began to place the gauze on his face and cocked an eyebrow at him. It was like, to her it should've been obvious, but Sam was clueless.

"It's not." She stood up. "It was good seeing you, Samual."

"Wait—you're leaving?"

"Yes, I'm going home. I'm tired." The matter-of-factness in her voice upset him. He wasn't sure if he was upset at her or himself. Of course, she's tired. She just finished a shift at work, but he hadn't seen her in so long.

"Why?" he asked desperately.

"Why what?" Another valid response. Samual was confused, but he knew what he wanted, so he persisted.

"Why are you being this way? I haven't seen or heard from you in weeks. I'm up every morning expecting you to be at my door, but you're not. Did I do something wrong? How can I fix it? Are you avoiding me?" His sudden outburst was enough to attract the attention of the people around them.

Bleeding man on the street, and no one bats an eye. But the minute he starts arguing with her . . .

Samantha shook her head.

"Walk with me." She turned to walk away. Samual shamefully followed like a sad puppy. Most of the journey to their destination was an exercise in silence. Sam felt like he was walking to his execution. All the women shot him a look of anger as if they all understood he had pissed Samantha off, and the men gave their nods, understanding his pain. She had politely waited until no one was around before speaking.

"I can see why they call you StormBOY." The name never hurt so much. It was a lengthy walk before they reached their destination. It was a run-down apartment building. Judging from where he was in the city, the trip to the convenience store was at least a good twenty-minute walk out of their way.

Did she go out of her way like that for me?

It was a communal apartment complex. Everyone had to have the key to the door that let them into the building. There were a couple of guys out front hanging out drinking out of a paper bag.

"What's up, Sam?" One of the guys heckled Samantha, stumbling over himself, "This your new boy toy?"

"He wishes," she responded. Samual glared at them through his gauzed eye as they burst into laughter. If only they knew what he could do to them. They entered the building; half the lights were out, and pieces of the stripped wallpaper that lined the halls were either missing or beginning to peel off. This wasn't anything like how he'd imagined her life being. This place was nearly condemned. They finally arrived at the door, and she quickly unlatched her three locks before pushing the door open to her private space. It was like stepping into an alternate dimension. Everything was immaculate! She turned on the lights and it was as if she was lighting up new universes in this tiny space. Samual looked all over for any sort of imperfection, but there was none to be found.

"Shoes."

Samual followed her instructions immediately.

"Sit!"

Again, following orders, Sam sat down and waited. Samantha let out one big stretch and disappeared into the kitchen. It felt like an ambush. At any point, he would need to unleash his powers on those lying in wait to get the drop on him.

No, that's stupid. It's Sam. She wouldn't do that to me! What am I thinking?

She reemerged suddenly, and Samual straightened in his chair immediately. A small burst of electricity leapt out of his body, causing the lamp next to him to flicker before returning to full brightness.

"You OK?" Samantha said, cocking her eye yet again. She glared at him suspiciously. His shirt now clung to his torso from the static he was emitting. He awkwardly kept trying to pull it off himself as he smiled nervously. She brought a bottle of red wine and poured each of them a glass. "Drink!"

Sam was nervous. He had never really drunk anything like this before.

"Do I have to?"

"You wanted to talk, so yes! Drink!" Samual obeyed, surprised to find that it was sweeter than he had imagined. As she enjoyed her beverage, Samantha kept an eye on him to make sure he had been drinking as well. Samual had attempted to put the drink down, but she placed her hand on the underside of his glass and forced him to continue.

"Are you happy now?" Sam gasped. He wiped the bits of liquid that poured down the sides of his mouth. She had just finished her glass as well.

"Not yet." She smiled and reached for the bottle again. Sam had wondered if Freight Train had a lesson for this as well.

"Do I have to drink this, too?"

"Yes, I want you to be honest for this conversation!" she replied.

Have I been dishonest?

He had now been halfway through his second drink, and his head felt foggy. Thoughts went directly to any sort of lesson Mr. Kain had taught him.

"You are trying to poison me!"

She laughed. "In a sense."

Samual looked at the drink and raised it to his mouth and downed the rest of it in one gulp. Samantha's face grew concerned.

"So, you going to talk to me now?" Samual reeled back and relaxed on the couch. He pulled one last time on his shirt, becoming less and less concerned about its clinginess.

"That guy got you pretty good," she said. Samual touched his face. He had almost forgotten it was there.

"It's OK. I had a pretty good nurse." He smiled at her, but she wasn't having it.

"How often do you come home looking like this?"

"I don't know," Sam responded. "Sometimes there are good nights and sometimes they aren't."

"That's it?"

"It's the job. What am I supposed to do?"

"What if one day you're out there and you get hurt? Not a scratch on the face or a black eye, but really hurt, and no one is around to help you. Then what?"

Sam paused.

"I die?"

The air grew stale. Sam had known he had crossed a line, but the words just spilled right out of him.

"Oh, is that all?" Her voice sounded distant.

"Freight Train was . . ." he paused again. "Everything for them."

That triggered her. Samantha had gotten up swiftly and stomped out of the room. Samual stood to follow but lost his balance and sat right back down.

What does she want from me?

She eventually reemerged, dressed a lot more casually. She had changed out of her fitted scrubs and now had on some shorts and a loose fitted tank top, which was the color of a sunflower. She was just finishing putting her hair in a ponytail. There was nothing extravagant about what she was wearing, but Samual's face still grew hot.

"Tell me something, Sam." she said, lowering her hands. "Before you were Stormboy, who were you?"

"What do you mean?"

"Before all this happened to you. You had to have been someone. Like as a kid, before the Maverick of Westside was born."

"Maverick of Westside?"

"That's what they are calling you now." She pointed at a tabloid on the coffee table. Sure enough, the cover had a crude drawing of a mugshot of him with that very title. He had tried to think. It was hard to recall much before Mr. Kain. All those unpleasant memories . . . he did his best to forget. All the training in the rubber room, and of course, all the people he hurt. Everything before Stormboy was painful.

"What does it matter?" Sam said, trying his best to dismiss the question entirely. These things shouldn't concern him.

"It matters to me." Samantha's face became distraught. Why was it that every time he spoke to her, it made her mad? He wanted to fix it, wanted to see her smile, but the right words eluded him. "It's like every time you talk to me, you aren't the one who's speaking. I want to know what you think!"

"I'm sorry." It was all he could muster. Samantha had poured herself another glass of wine and gestured if he wanted some, too. He was nervous to accept, but also didn't want to disappoint her again. She filled his glass once more. Sam stared at his reflection in the liquid.

Why am I even here right now? I'm only going to hurt her. Connections are cancer.

He had to say something.

"I guess what I want to say is, I honestly don't remember. My life has been Stormboy, and anything else was just . . . let's just say, being a foster child who could fry your entire block's electrical grid wasn't the easiest."

Samantha stared intently. She made her way over and sat beside him once again. Samual had taken another sip of his glass and continued.

"I wasn't afforded the luxury of being me. I always had to be the one that people wanted. Whenever a potential parent came around, you had to put on a performance. But as time went on and people found out what I was, even that wouldn't work. No one wanted me. No one wants a freak. Well, no one except Mr. Kain."

"You mean Freight Train," Samantha said. Sam nodded.

"I'm Stormboy because I have never been anyone else." Sam looked down at his cup, not realizing that through telling his story he had made it through half of the glass of wine. He set it down and stood, being extra careful not to trip over himself again. He allowed the world to settle, as it now tended to want to spin. Suddenly, lightning began to emanate and dance all over his body. It tangled around him like snakes wrapping around one another. "Mr. Kain taught me how to control this. He taught me how to use this curse and make it so I could help people with it. He's given me everything, and I could never repay him enough for that."

"You respect him a lot, don't you?" Samantha asked. He nodded back sheepishly.

"He was my father, and he needed me to be Stormboy, so that's who I am."

There he was. A child again. Ready to cry over the man. He let the storm settle. Samantha had sat there with one leg up, which she rested her arm on, that arm holding her cocked head. She wasn't quite staring at Sam, but just passed him. It was incredible how used to the storm she was now. Or maybe the wine had made it so she hadn't noticed. Either way, Sam was transfixed on her as she began to speak.

"I never loved my father, not really. He always loved telling Mom what to do." Her face became stiff as a board. It gave off the impression that she wasn't sure if she wanted to keep drinking or curse really loud. "I didn't agree with her, but I understood her. My mother grew up in a different time. She didn't work, never finished school. She knew what she was, and that was dad's wife, nothing else."

Her eyes glazed as she began to recount her tale. She had taken center stage, with her pristine white walls sitting on her couch and her beautiful caramel skin. It was as if Sam had fallen into a painting. Her beauty swallowed everything around her. Nothing else in the world mattered to him at this moment but what she had to say. Her story obviously made her uncomfortable, so she readjusted herself and crossed her arms before continuing.

"I was the only girl besides Mom in a house full of men, so certain things were expected of me. Mom taught me the proper way to be a 'lady,' but that's not who I wanted to be. But I had to do what I had to do or else mom would suffer for it." Her arms went up in air quotes to exaggerate certain points in her story. Samantha had always been so jovial and innocent; never once did he think she could've grown up with any hardship. It made him feel like an idiot. "I always hated her for letting Dad do that to her. All the times he would have to 'put her in her place,' as he said. She seemed so confident and bright in front of my brothers, even behind all the bruises. But when we were alone . . ." She paused. Her eyes drifted to Samual for the first time since she had begun speaking but quickly sank right back to her glass.

"You know one time, when my father and brothers were at a football game, she showed me that she had this art collection. At first, I figured it was things she bought behind Daddy's back, but of course not; she didn't have the nerve to do that. She actually painted everything herself. Paintings of families in the parks she used to take us to or open fields where lovers would caress. All of them were so beautiful. When I asked her who had seen them, I remember her frowning and saying just me. I told her we could try selling them, to let the world see her gift! But she refused. She was a mother, after all, she said. What more could she possibly be? I love my mother more than anything in the world! But I swore that day that I would never be like her!"

She wiped her eyes preemptively for tears.

"I told my parents I was going away to school to be a nurse. I had gotten a scholarship and worked my ass off so I wouldn't have to ask them for anything. I wanted to show Daddy that I didn't need him and to show Mom that I'd be OK on my own. I could take my father's tantrums; I had seen that my entire life. All the cursing and the insults he gave me meant nothing. I remember all the shouting. 'Why didn't you marry that doctor boy?' and 'A woman's place is at home with her family.' It was all nonsense that I could get over. What killed me was the look on Mom's face. On the day I left, I remember her eyes. I couldn't tell if she was proud that I was escaping or upset that I was leaving her behind. I tried to stay in touch, but over the years, they slowly stopped taking my calls. That was three years ago now."

"Do you ever regret leaving her?" Sam finally said.

"Not for a second. There are nights when I miss her. But I made a promise that I wouldn't be like her. So here I am."

Samual looked around at her home. The pristine nature of it all now was clear to him. It was a statement. A testament to her independence. She gently fondled her locket around her neck.

"But don't you ever . . ." He hesitated. Even in this immensely vulnerable moment she gave him, she seemed so sure of herself. He didn't want to mess this up.

"Sam," she spoke. "Are you happy?"

"I am." He was looking directly into her eyes. Every word he spoke after this moment was critical. He wanted so much to be with her all the time even though everything he did and said around her felt so death-defying.

"Are you?" She gestured to him to join her on the couch. She summoned, and he obeyed.

"I am right now." Sam felt relief. At this moment right now. He felt good. Better than he had ever felt before.

"But when you leave here, how will you feel?" her hands

cupped his on his lap.

"I don't know . . . I haven't left yet."

"You're impossible!" She violently squeezed his hands before letting him go.

"What do you want me to say? Sure, sometimes I feel alone and angry. But this is who I am, and this is all I have." He whipped his hand up in a fist and lightning began to orbit it. "I don't have any other options. This is what I was raised to be, and that's it! This is who I have to be . . . right?"

The outburst had taken a lot out of him. Everything felt sincere, but he was still surprised his mouth spilled that last word.

This is all I can be. Everything for them. Right?

He was breathing quite heavily now, waiting for her to respond.

"Stay right here." Samantha shot up and pranced to the other room. He had just had an outburst. His emotions got the better of him, and she hadn't run away or scolded him. It made him worry more that she hadn't. Life had been so much simpler just a month ago. Wake up, catch some bad guy, go to sleep, and repeat. Mr. Kain's words had made so much sense before, but now?

Samantha returned. It was another wardrobe change. She had now sported tight black leggings and a T-shirt that said "Just deal with it" in bold graffiti. She had let her hair down and was combing it into submission, no doubt knotted from the bun and ponytail she had it in prior. She had a smile on her face.

"Finish that and come with me."

Samual swished back his drink and took her hand as she led him out of the apartment and into the city streets. The world had fallen away. All that was left was his hand holding hers. They moved so swiftly that between his rapture and the wine, his vision was having a hard time keeping up. While she maneuvered him through the streets, his mind fixated on her words to him.

What am I doing? What do I actually want?

"Check it out!" They had finally made it. Sam had finally gotten his bearings.

"City hall," he said. The front of city hall was made entirely of glass, only obscured by the large support columns.

"Isn't it gorgeous? This is my favorite place in the city!" Samantha had turned her head and got her answer from Samual's expression.

"Did you know this was the fifth building they constructed after founding this city? Alexander West made sure that everything outside to the columns inside was perfectly symmetrical. It reminds me of the Taj Mahal. Not to that scale, but obviously, the beauty in the order of it all is astounding."

His knowledge of the building caught Samantha off guard, but she listened intently as Sam gushed on. He didn't often get to talk to anyone about his knowledge of the buildings in Westside.

"And with its large glass front, everyone, no matter what time of day, could look inside and see the portrait of the founding day of the city."

The sun had begun to go down, but it was still light enough to illuminate a massive portrait inside the building. Mounted behind a reception desk, the portrait depicted a massive party and ribbon-cutting ceremony on the very block they were on. His mouth was a broken fire hydrant, spouting random facts about the building. Any inhibition he once felt flew out the window. He wanted to shut up, but he also wanted to tell her about the idea behind the glass front of the building and how the founders believed that all politics that ran through city hall should be one hundred percent transparent to its people. He explained the design inspiration for all the neighboring buildings as well as any major historical moments regarding the story of the city of Westside until his mouth went dry.

"I'm sorry." he said sheepishly.

"For what?"

"I kind of got caught up."

"Yeah, you did!" Samantha laughed, and Samual flushed. "I'm glad."

"Can I take you to my favorite place?" he said.

"The night is young, Stormboy." Samual's face soured at the name. Samantha did her best to contain her laughter. He extended his hand to meet hers, and when they finally touched, a tiny shock was exchanged between them. Samantha's hand recoiled for a second, but Samual didn't let her escape. They both smiled as he guided her once again through the city.

They made their way downtown, which was as alive as ever! Samantha had begged him to stop for just a moment as she approached a duet. A violinist and a guitarist playing a beautiful symphony together. It had seemed she knew the violinist and dropped some money into her case. The music they had played was spectacular, nothing like Samual had ever heard before; that's when he caught eye with the guitarist. Anton, the kid from the abandoned movie theater that night, with his eyes closed, vibing to every strum on his guitar, only opening his eyes occasionally, to stare at his partner.

Good job, buddy.

"Come on. We are running out of time." Samual smiled. Samantha nodded and took his hand to follow.

"I wish we could come back and listen to them sometime! Their playing was so beautiful!"

"We will one day. I promise."

Where he wanted to take her was on the other side of town. The darker side. Many of the lights in this area were broken or no longer working, but he still guided her. He could tell she was getting a bit nervous.

"It's OK. I'm a superhero, remember?"

Sam guided her to a fire escape, and they made their way to the rooftop. They were cutting it close on time. The sun was getting lower and lower in the sky.

"Are we even allowed to be up here?" Samantha asked. She

gazed back and forth nervously, but was still obviously very excited.

"It's almost time," he replied to her. He took her hand and eased her down to sit on the edge of the building. The sky glowed a fiery red as the last bits of the sun from the day caught the new night sky. "This is my favorite time of day."

"Most people enjoy sunsets," she said, mocking him. He ignored the slight and gestured to her to look out toward the city. It was the starting point of route six of his patrols. Stormboy saw it as the beginning of a night of work, but Samual saw it as something else entirely.

"You ready?" he asked. He raised his hand and began to countdown. "Five, four, three, two . . ."

The sun dipped below the horizon, and like a flood from behind them, the automated streetlights lit the entire city. There had been some dark spots in some of the lower-income areas, but other than that, the entire city looked like it had been lit on fire!

"It looks like Tenth and Jefferson needs some attention." He pointed toward one of the darker areas. "And Fifth through Seventh have been out for some time now, but still . . . it's a whole new city!"

They both sat there and let it all soak in. For all the nastiness and evil he had dealt with on a day-to-day basis, it was moments like this where he looked out and it appeared Westside was straight out of a fairy tale. Samantha hadn't said a word.

"Do you like it?" he asked.

"It's beautiful Sam." Her words barely escaped her mouth.

"This city is something else."

"It sure is." This time, she sounded almost sad. And before he realized it, she had gotten up and was walking away. Samual turned to see her massaging her elbows. "Can you take me home? I'm getting cold."

The sun had just set, and it hadn't had time to get cold yet, but Samual knew better than to protest.

"Sure." He sprang back to his feet and followed Samantha close behind. They walked so closely together that their strides would occasionally cause them to bump shoulders.

"Is everything OK?" He had to ask.

"I really don't want to talk about it," she said.

"Why not?" Samual pondered out loud. "I thought we were doing so well." He didn't even know what he meant by that. Like she was some sort of task that he could pass or fail.

"I mean, not well. Well, I mean." Samual stopped in the middle of the sidewalk and slapped his forehead. Her previously abrasive demeanor loosened as she let out a chuckle.

"Don't worry. You are doing very well." Her smile was electric. He had recognized this smile. The bank tellers and their families, the couple in the alley, Anton and Nikki. The smile that loved ones shared with one another. A smile he always wanted for himself.

Alas, their trek finally led to outside her building once more. The guys hanging out front were long gone, only empty bottles and the lingering stench of cigarettes loomed in the air now. She rustled for her keys and leaned against her building's entrance.

"So?" her head hit the glass with a tiny thud, harder than Samual was sure she meant.

"So," he echoed. Every interaction had been a calculated risk. She pushed herself off the wall. Her beautiful brown eyes, completely darkened now, had danced around the floor to Sam and back again.

"You OK?" he asked.

"Yeah. You need to stop asking that." Her face poured into a smile, finally showing her teeth. Samual wanted to leap into the air for a moment. "I think I finally know who you are."

"What do you mean?"

"I know who Samual is." His heart stopped at her words. Whether it was from happiness or reservation, he couldn't tell, but Samual hung on every word.

"And who is that?"

"You are a boy."

Samual cocked his head in confusion at her words.

"You know who you are and what you want, but you are waiting for someone to give you permission to be that person."

A boy!

Samantha continued.

"You're kind and sweet, but out of a sense of duty or some personal code. And you care." She broke up her last sentence. She could tell Samual wasn't taking it too well. "You care so much, but it's like it's because some personal responsibility has been thrust upon you."

It was as if he had been punched in the chest by Freight Train himself.

"I'm sorry, was that too much?" She leaned in to grasp the expression on his face.

"So, you don't think I care about you?" Samual was mortified.

"I don't know. I hope so."

A needle stuck into his chest, and his blood began to run hot. He could feel it from his toes to the back of his eyes. The wound on his face felt like it would split open.

"Good night, Stormboy."

When he finally snapped out of it, she was right up against his unscarred cheek and gave it a soft kiss. His emotions confused him. He wanted to say something, anything, to defend himself. Words escaped him.

Everything for them!

Samual closed his eyes to fight back the tears. He raised his face to meet hers, but what he was met with was a closing door. Just like that, she was gone. He stood there alone for a moment, and then another moment. On his third moment, he let out a faint whisper.

"Good night."

CHAPTER 9

TIME TO BE A HERO

Why does everything feel so bright?

Samual sat in his bed the next morning paralyzed. His eyes fixated on the ceiling in one specific spot, but that spot danced around, making it hard to focus on. Despite feeling that the sun was literally inside his room, Sam couldn't help but think about last night. How wonderful it had been, and how that wonder had ended so abruptly. But these thoughts also ended abruptly as his insides demanded to be outside.

He had never felt so useless in his entire life. Everything he ate his body rejected, any time he moved, he immediately found the floor instead. It was agony. The only thing that felt right was sleep. Within these moments of unconsciousness, his mind trailed back to the early days. He and Freight Train fighting side by side, stopping bad guys and having that sense of accomplishment that came with every victim saved. He looked up at that smiling face of Mr. Kain, but something felt off. When he peered out at the crowd of citizens he was smiling at, all their faces were melted and smeared as if they were the edge of a candle. All of them simultaneously looked at Stormboy, with their molded indented faces, and began to applaud him. Stormboy looked up at Mr. Kain, but he had not changed, his hands firmly on his hips, chest puffed out, and laughing as if he told a great joke that the world was now congratulating him on. All the wax people homed in on Stormboy, staring with their featureless faces. The space where their eyes should be staring into his soul.

Clap. Clap. Clap.

They all walked and clapped in unison. Stormboy tried to back away but stumbled directly into Freight Train. There was nowhere to run. The clapping turned to screaming and, one by one, the wax-faced citizens fell to the floor, convulsing violently in agony. Stormboy looked down at his hands. His power flared uncontrollably through them. He begged Freight Train to help him, but he remained motionless, frozen in that same sense of triumph. The waxed-faced citizens were on top of him now and his body did the only thing it knew how to do. A torrent of electricity shot out in every direction launching all those around him.

Samual awoke soon after in a pool of his own sweat. The ceiling had stopped spinning, and the only thing left was fear. Nightmares were not new, but nothing was ever so intense. He made a quick trip to the refrigerator to hydrate himself. He couldn't seem to escape the vision he had just seen. He grabbed his hood and mask and made his way out onto the streets. The only way to keep his mind off it was to patrol. It was always his means of escape. The air that brushed his face as he leapt from the rooftops and the vision of the city was therapy to him. Even still, tonight still felt different. He couldn't shake the unsettling feeling. He took his usual patrol route number three, making sure to hit all the common spots that criminals of Westside liked to wander. Nothing!

If this were any other night, the streets would be crawling.

The horns of the traffic below howled across the night and the hustle of the city below became more apparent. Stormboy closed his eyes and covered his ears.

"Everything for them," he whispered to himself. Freight

Train entered his mind and his words sang in his head.

"Everything for them," he repeated to himself. "They are afraid of you."

No, not that one!

Sam's head began to fill with more and more of his mentor's proverbs that he was beginning to become overwhelmed.

"Keep calm and keep control!" Sparks of electricity spilled off him.

Breathe! Relax. There, that's it.

His powers subsided somewhat as he began to whisper to himself again.

"You're sweet and kind out of a sense of duty."

Wait—what?

Why was he thinking about her right now? He was slipping. Every word and mantra that Freight Train had ever taught him, and the words Samantha had said the night before now swam in his mind, all vying for his attention. When he couldn't take it anymore, he started to run. He hurtled across roof gaps for more blocks than he could keep track of. His regular routes be damned. He just needed to go somewhere, anywhere! His eyes darting in every direction, as if they were trying to escape his skull. He was running, but where was he going? He deviated from his route in desperation. There had to be someone somewhere that he could stop. He wanted to be Stormboy, so he didn't have to think about being Sam. When he couldn't run anymore, he fell to his knees and screamed. His talent surged wildly, coating the roof in their combined electric rage!

Breathe. You have to breathe.

The lightning surged relentlessly; he could feel it flowing off him.

You have to stop.

How many people could he hurt if he didn't get this under control?

Just breathe. Just stop! Please.

As if there were some silent agreement between him and the storm within him, the lightning began to subside. He heard shrieks and cries from the building below. No doubt he hurt someone in the building below. The amount of voltage he put out, someone had to have been caught up in the cross-fire. Not to mention all the electrical equipment he must have destroyed.

I have to get out of here.

Sam made a call to emergency services before heading off into Lowtown. He wished he could do something else for them, but he felt it better to just remove himself from the situation. Let the professionals handle it.

The buildings in Lowtown were, as the name implied, "low." Compared to the rest of Westside, these buildings seldom reached over three stories. He went to the edge of one of the rooftops and let his feet dangle off the side.

What am I doing?

The streets below were dark and quiet. It had been close to midnight, and it wasn't like downtown here. Most of the people were working class and had to be up early the next day. It was the best place to sit and relax.

Breathe.

He noticed four people rushing out of the corner store. They were scared, Stormboy realized, and he immediately leapt into action. Lightning sparked on him as if it were excited to finally see something happen.

Keep calm. They are more afraid of you than you are of them.

Freight Train's words came to him, and everything else fell silent. It was time to be Stormboy, finally. Time to be a hero!

When he made it to street level, Stormboy assessed the situation. The entire front of the shop was glass, but he still had a hard time seeing the inside of the store. Stormboy snuck to the front of the shop to try to peer through the entrance. There, he noticed a man holding a gun to the cashier. If he snuck into the shop, he could probably catch the guy off guard and incapacitate him before he ever had a chance to do any harm.

I guess I care more about Samual than Stormboy.

Stormboy let the lightning stream from his right index finger, up his back, and around to his other index finger.

Breathe.

In one swift motion, Stormboy swung the door open. The gunman turned around surprised, which left him wide open for a stream of the storm to fly right into his chest, sending him clear to the other side of the room.

"Are you hurt?" Stormboy said, as he allowed a ball of lightning to flare in his hand to illuminate the cashier's face. She was clearly horrified, crying her eyes out. She motioned to say something, but her fear had paralyzed her.

You are caring, but out of some sense of responsibility.

"Ma'am, you are going to be OK." Her cries wouldn't stop. He wanted to reach out and grab her hand, but she suddenly stiffened. Her voice trembled, and she raised her hand to point behind him.

"There are two . . ." Before she could finish, Stormboy heard a loud crack and felt a sudden heat in his stomach. He whipped his body around so fast he nearly fell over. The ball of lightning had faded, so he only caught a brief glimpse of the shooter's face. The pain he felt was overwhelming. His powers acted on instinct as he shot a hail of lightning in the shooter's general direction. The entire store lit up in an array of purple light as the streams connected with the shooter. All that was left was the sound of the cashier sobbing. Stormboy clenched his stomach and turned to her once more.

"No more?" It was all he could muster. She nodded. "Call the police!"

Stormboy burst out of the shop too afraid to look down at his wound. He tried to stay strong. The pain was excruciating, but he could not show weakness. As soon as he was out of view of the streets, he collapsed to one knee. Freight Train had to have something for this! He searched his thoughts, but everything led back to the pain. He finally removed his hand to reveal the severity of his circumstance. His hand was coated with blood. The realization of it all caused the storm in him to rage.

No, not now! Please. Not again.

Stormboy removed his mask and hood and discarded it in the nearby dumpster.

You have to stop! We need help. So, you have to stop now!

The storm began to subside. It was actually obeying him. Despite the overwhelming emotion he was feeling, the storm began to subside.

Samual got to his feet and began to make his way to the streets. He needed help, and he needed it soon. His undershirt was now soaked with blood.

Someone please . . . help me.

He finally reached the streets, where he fell out onto the sidewalk. It was quiet, as Lowtown typically was, but there was one citizen that rushed over.

"Hey buddy, are you OK?" The man said, swinging a guitar onto his back. Sam wanted to respond but couldn't find it in him. This was it. Not a rousing battle, but a bullet in the back. His legs curled in as close to his chest as his wound allowed. He was now spilling out onto the pavement, and his mind went silent.

CHAPTER 70

WESTSIDE GENERAL

His breathing was weak, but steady. Samual couldn't understand why it took so long to open his eyes, but he did so as soon as he was able. The light that poured in from the window was too bright to deal with, so he turned his head. A long white curtain which accentuated the sunshine flowed on his right.

What happened? Where am I?

He looked down at his stomach and was immediately reminded. The corner store, the girl, and the shooter. He remembered lights flashing and the sound like thunder booming in his head so loud it made him wince. The machine next to him, which emitted a low rhythmic beeping, became louder and more frantic. He remembered the convulsing body and all the lightning he had poured into the man with the gun. The memory horrified him. All of which was amplified by the sound of the crying girl.

Oh God!

The beeping became out of control like it was screaming in pain. Suddenly, an older gentleman entered the room and urgently moved to Sam's side.

"Son, please, you need to calm down!" Samual gazed into

his eyes. His thick-rimmed glasses reflected Sam's exasperated expression back to him. Sam did his best to lie back in the bed while the doctor adjusted some levers on the tubes behind him.

"What did I do?" He could feel the storm brewing in him. "Where is . . ."

"My boy, please. I'm more worried about you at the moment."

Sam needed to relax. His stomach felt like it was on fire. If he carried on like this, he may not be able to control the storm.

We had an agreement. Stay calm! Breathe.

The machine began to slow and with it the storm in him as well.

"You want to tell me what happened to you?" The doctor asked calmly. He didn't, but no one walked into the hospital with a bullet wound and walked out without some sort of explanation.

"A kid had a gun, got antsy, and I was in the way," he said, praying he would buy that story.

"You were lucky someone was able to get you to us when they did! The bullet caught you good. We were able to stop the bleeding in time, any longer out there and . . ."

The doctor trailed off, afraid to finish his sentence.

"So, you're saying I'm going to be OK?" Sam responded.

"What I'm saying is that you are very lucky." The doctor tucked the clipboard into a pouch at the end of the bed. "You should be more careful. Maybe try to stay out of the way next time. Stormboy and the police can't be everywhere, you know."

The doctor flipped the switch on the television in the room. The news was broadcasting a face he instantly recognized. How could he get that girl's face out of his head?

"He came in and took out the two guys like they were nothing!" The girl explained, short of breath, to the news reporter.

"But he used his abilities on one of the robbers and killed him, isn't that right?" the reporter protested.

"Well yes, but . . ." The girl tried to speak but was immediately cut off.

"You heard it here, citizens of Westside. Stormboy, the vigilante, claims another victim, bringing his death and injury total to six this fateful night. When will city hall wake up and do something about the menace of Westside?"

Sam sucked his teeth. He was pissed at the negative press, but they were right. Six people killed or injured in one night was unacceptable. He knew by losing control of his emotions on that rooftop he would hurt someone. He failed. He hurt people again!

"Those men were going to kill me!" The girl spoke up and pushed her way back into the frame. "Even though he was hurt, Stormboy managed to save me. I honestly just hope he's OK! Thank you, Stormboy!"

The girl's eyes flushed with tears, and she stared into the camera, as if speaking directly to him. The newscasters had suddenly switched to their typical crime statistics and analytics on Stormboy's presence in the neighborhood, completely ignoring the girl's statement. It was exactly the kind of stuff that made him stay away from the news and their reporters. They had gone on and on with numbers, trying to spin a story that he had been causing more harm than good, but this time it didn't matter. He had managed to save that girl's life, and that's what mattered.

What if you get hurt and you're all alone?

The doctor was right, after all. He was lucky. He imagined the worst-case scenario; his heart began to race again.

"Easy, son. You're all right now." The doctor turned a valve on a tube that Sam had noticed now was connected to his arm. His breathing began to slow, and his eyes became too heavy to bear anymore. The doctor whispered something to him, but he could not understand. His body relaxed for a moment; he blinked and suddenly he was on a rooftop.

"I'm getting too old for this shit." A familiar-sounding voice appeared behind him. Mr. Kain had taken to saying that more and more toward the end. With a quick stretch of his back, he perched next to Stormboy. Freight Train was in his uniform. Solid grey shirt with his signature train insignia and close-fitting slacks. He had claimed he did not want any loose clothes, but Stormboy knew it was because he was proud of his muscular figure and knew his enemies would fear him more if they could see the extent of his physique. Stormboy rolled his eyes. He held his head again. Another symptom of old age, Stormboy thought. He always seemed a little out of it these days.

"Maybe you should have stayed home then," Stormboy said, with a bit of snark. He must've been, at most, twenty-two at this point. Sam remembered this night all too well. This was their last night out together.

"What, and let you have all the fun?" Freight Train retorted with a snicker.

"Is that what you call it?"

"Of course. What would you call it?"

"Work!" Stormboy gazed into his binoculars, fixated on a storage unit they had been tracking for months. His focus kept darting from his binoculars to his watch and back again. "Looks like you should've stayed home, Pops! Nothing is happening here. Maybe you could do something about these little headaches of yours."

"My head is fine! When did you get so impatient? He starts working alone and, all of a sudden, he's big time!" Freight Train snagged the binoculars from him. "You should relax a little bit. What's the rush? Got a hot date?"

Stormboy shoved off to go sit on an AC vent.

"I could be out there doing something else. What if someone is out there that needs one of us, and we are here sitting on our butts doing nothing? This is a waste of time!"

Freight Train straightened up and turned to Stormboy quickly and sternly. "Hey, you need to calm down right now. Do your breathing exercise."

"I don't need to . . ." Freight Train gave a look, and Stormboy knew it was best he just shut up and do the exercise. He allowed his powers to surge. Streaks of lightning flew toward the electrical boxes and streetlamps all around the building every time he breathed in and out. All control, all calmness. He felt at peace with himself and his abilities every time he did it. He had seen his powers as a curse before all this, but now when he did his exercise, the beast had been leashed. It made him feel stupid for lashing out. Mr. Kain had always been right about the breathing exercise. Every time he thought he didn't need it anymore, Mr. Kain always told him to do it, and he was always right.

Why was he always right?

Stormboy's mind wandered to all the times he had been out on the streets with Freight Train, the countless stakeouts, all the criminals they had put away, and yet here they were, out again, another stakeout, another criminal, another breathing exercise. It all felt futile. A never-ending crusade. He wondered if . . .

"Bingo!" Even his whispers had a strong sense of authority around them. "Come here, boy!"

Stormboy allowed his ability to fade and quickly joined his mentor. Freight Train passed him the binoculars and pointed off into the distance. About three blocks away, several cars were pulling into an abandoned warehouse. There were armed thugs making their way out of a van carrying large sacks of God knows what. Some even had to pair up to carry some of the larger cases. This was the reason they were here. This is what Freight Train had been waiting on. One quick look at him and he was certain that was true.

"All right! Let's go bust up some bad guys!"

Before Stormboy could respond, Freight Train leapt off

the building to the ground. He paused for a moment, his head a little rattled before taking off into a sprint.

I hate it when he does this!

Stormboy rushed to the nearest fire escape, jumping down the steps loudly and feverishly in a desperate attempt to catch up. By the looks of these guys, they meant business. The firearms they were handling were nothing like Stormboy was used to. By the time he had finally reached him, Freight Train was poised at a favorable distance from the thugs in the warehouse. He was in the middle of his pre-fight ritual. A man of habit, as always. He cracked each finger individually, then his wrists, elbows, neck, and finally knees.

"Wait!" Stormboy exclaimed.

"What's the problem now?"

"Didn't you see how many there were in there?"

"What does that matter?" Freight Train's dismissiveness made Stormboy even more uncomfortable, "With my strength and your 'zappiness,' they don't stand a chance."

"They have guns! And not just regular handguns! A lot of crazy big guns, and a lot of people shooting those guns!"

"I don't understand. We are heroes! We are only going to get one shot at this, who knows where this stuff is going after tonight!" Freight Train resumed his trek toward the warehouse, followed reluctantly by his ward.

"All I'm saying is this doesn't seem like a run in and beat 'em all up kind of job."

"What are you suggesting, then?" Freight Train was growing impatient.

"I don't know. Strategy maybe?"

"Strategy?" Freight Train approached a nearby parked car and lifted it over his head. "Who needs strategy when you can do this?"

He wasn't reaching him.

He never listens to me.

"There are a lot of people in there, a lot of armed people,

and I know you say they are more scared of us than we are of them, but . . ." Freight Train put the car down and knelt down next to him. "I'm scared, sir."

Freight Train sighed heavily and massaged the bridge of his nose.

"We've done this for so long now. You have to believe in yourself and what you are capable of. You've come so far. You are practically a pro!"

Stormboy sunk into himself, and Freight Train moved to comfort him.

"So, strategy, huh? What did you have in mind?"

It was three in the morning and the two guards stood at their post in the warehouse for what felt like an eternity. The streets were quiet—disturbingly so.

"Why we even gotta be here, man?" Marcus wore a black long-sleeved sweater with black jeans. He had anticipated a cold front that never came, and now he was just uncomfortable. Between his attire and the rifle he had been holding for the past four hours, he was ready to abandon his post and take a nice, cold shower. "Them bitches in there need to hurry up. I ain't tryin' to be out here all night!"

The second thug scoffed. He wore a close-fitting shirt with a tattoo that peaked out from under his left sleeve. From the way he carried himself, he seemed to be ex-military.

"This is the job. Don't get antsy," the soldier remarked.

"I ain't antsy."

"Really? Because you seem antsy."

The two flanked the warehouse door they had been charged with protecting. They had associates inside conducting "business," whatever the hell that meant. All Marcus knew was that it was good money for one night's work, and he could certainly use the money. But what the hell could they possibly be doing in there for so long?

"I don't like it, man!" Marcus said finally.

"Just shut up, keep your eyes open, and collect the god-damn money." The soldier spoke in a confident assertiveness.

"Do you know where we are, man? This is Westside! If we are here too long, we got a chance of running into him!"

"Just stay focused," the soldier said. Marcus was broke, but he wasn't dumb. He knew the kind of stuff that happened in Westside. He clutched his weapon tight; the two began their patrols in opposite directions. Marcus reached the end of the warehouse, peered around the corner and along the east end of the warehouse lot. Silence.

"This is pointless, man! We should get out of here." Marcus turned back around to meet his partner, but he was slumped over on the floor. Marcus pulled his gun to the ready as he approached his downed partner.

"Hey! You good?" he shouted. The man remained motion-less. He saw a large hole in the wall above the downed soldier; someone had punched straight through it. "I know you're here Freight Train! Show yourself!" Marcus swung his gun around feverishly, as every slight sound in the lot was now a threat. He approached the other side of the warehouse. Still silence. But when he turned, he saw a young man he didn't recognize standing in front of him.

"You ain't Freight Train," Marcus said confused.

"Nope."

Suddenly, Marcus could feel every nerve ending in his body fighting him at once. His entire body betrayed him as he fell to the ground.

Freight Train emerged from the shadows.

"So. Strategy, huh?"

Stormboy smiled out of the side of his mouth as his men-tor patted him on the back.

Inside the warehouse was a huge room filled with old con-struction equipment and machinery. In the center of the room laid two long tables where several men were shouting over each other.

"So where do we go from here, boy?" Freight Train questioned as the two positioned themselves behind an old bulldozer. The two of them scoped out the interior of the warehouse. Besides the men in the center of the room, there were others lining a catwalk that stretched around the edges of the building with a bridge going across the center.

I could only imagine what would've happened if we had come in with the original plan.

There were so many of them. At the mere sight of all the thugs, Stormboy's chest tightened. He couldn't help it. His legs slid from under him, and his butt made a thud onto the floor.

"Whoa, whoa! What's wrong?" Freight Train's eager smile faded into concern for his ward.

"I can't do this, sir!" Stormboy's hands had now firmly clutched his chest. Freight Train knelt next to him and placed his large leaden hand on his shoulder. He had handled criminals before, but this was practically an army!

"You can. You are stronger than you give yourself credit for."

It felt as if he was pushing him into the floor.

"But . . ." he trailed off, failing to hold the tears in his eyes. Crying was for children, and he wasn't a child anymore, but still they came. "There are so many of them. What if I get hurt or worse? What if I hurt them?"

Freight Train only smiled.

"That's exactly what makes you fit to do this."

Stormboy looked at the man, confused.

"You know your own strength, but you still use it to protect people. Like a hero would."

His smile was so reassuring. It was the face of the man the city grew to trust, the face of the man who now put that same trust in him. Stormboy wiped his tears away.

Breathe.

"You ready?" Freight Train asked, presenting his hand to help him to his feet. Stormboy nodded. "Let's get this done and go home!"

In one swift motion, Stormboy was back on his feet and ready for anything. Freight Train jumped over the bulldozer they hid behind and into clear view of the warehouse.

"Party time is over, boys!" Freight Train exclaimed.

Time seemed to stop. All the thugs' eyes now fixated on him.

"It's Freight Train. Kill him!" The warehouse was instantaneously riddled with gunfire, and Freight Train began to do what he did best.

So much for strategy!

The bullets just bounced off him. He gave little grunts almost as if he were being pelted with pebbles. Stormboy, however, stayed behind and took a moment to gather himself. He allowed his power to surge.

Breathe.

He kept repeating it over and over in his head.

"OK . . . Let's do this," he said aloud. Stormboy emerged from his hiding spot and began flinging bolts of lightning toward the thugs in the catwalk. They would be the hardest for Freight Train to deal with, so he figured it would be best to take them out first. Just because Freight Train didn't have a plan didn't mean he couldn't. He took a minute to survey the room before ducking back into cover, just in time, too, as a hail of bullets headed in his direction.

"Dammit, the kid is with him, too!" One of the gunmen shouted. Stormboy waited for this moment to reemerge; the chaos of the fight was overwhelming. He knew Freight Train would do everything in his power to keep the attention on him. He just had to wait long enough for them to readjust their focus. Stormboy let out more streams as he eliminated the men on the catwalk. It was going better than he had expected. He repeated this tactic, making sure he was constantly on the move whenever he could, when he noticed some were running for the exit. They were winning! The room was clearing, and Stormboy felt more comfortable staying out to take down four or five guys before he returned to the shadows.

"You had enough yet, boys?" Freight Train let out an exhausted scream. He stood tall and confident, but Stormboy knew he was pushing his limits. Those stupid headaches really took a lot out of him recently. "I can do this all day!"

Stormboy took stock of the situation; it was a near rout. Stormboy took some shots to stop those trying to escape, but wasn't able to stop all of them. But still, they managed to take out twenty at least, just the two of them. Was this what Freight Train meant all this time? All the confidence he had and the faith he placed in him. Freight Train's laugh had echoed through the building and his confidence was beginning to rub off on him.

The moment was fleeting, however. On one side of the warehouse, a garage door crumbled. One of the thugs had gotten a van from outside and burst back into the building. Before he could react, the van came careening into Freight Train, knocking him clear off his feet and into the opposite wall. Stormboy looked on in horror. Freight Train remained motionless on the floor.

"Don't forget the other one." The words echoed through the now silent warehouse, and it had knocked sense back into him, and he hid again behind some bullet-ridden crates.

No!

"Come out, Stormboy!" someone screamed. He tried to make himself as little as possible. "We promise it'll only hurt for a moment."

He needed a plan, and he needed it now! By the sound of their mocking laughter, they were getting closer. Stormboy squeezed his head, trying his best to keep focus.

Everything for them. No—shut up! That doesn't help right now!

"You guys are kidding yourselves; you know?" One of the thugs shouted, the echoes carrying throughout the warehouse. He could hear some other thugs kicking and mocking his downed mentor. "You really think you and your daddy are changing anything? You guys are a joke!"

He was out of time. It's now or never!

Please save us.

His talent raged out of him ferociously. A torrent of electricity filling the entire building.

"Leave him alone!" Stormboy frantically sprinted toward the pinned Freight Train. Anyone who dared to get near him was blown away with a spear of his talent through their chest. The bright flashes mixed with the tears and rage, which made him numb. All he knew was Freight Train needed help. Nothing else mattered. He thrusted his hands forward, and the whites and purples of his talent made it so bright that he couldn't look on in front of him without straining his eyes. His power had taken care of everything for him. All he needed to do was focus on getting to Freight Train. He felt a jubilance that he could only attribute to his talent being unleashed in such fervor. The energy flew out from every point in his body, all around the room, until the screaming eventually stopped, so it did as well. The carnage of it all left Stormboy stunned. So many bodies lay on the ground motionless. He collapsed onto his knees again next to his mentor, alone, until the police sirens cut through the warehouse. The officers came storming in through all available entrances like a swarm, but quickly relaxed upon seeing the massacre. The only one left sitting alone was a defeated Stormboy crying over a beaten and bloodied Freight Train.

"Son, are you OK?"

Stormboy forced his face to rise and meet the officers.

"We are going to need an ambulance."

CHAPTER 11

WHAT ABOUT ME?

Samual woke up in a pool of his own sweat. His eyes darted around the room frantically before realizing where he was. The white curtains, the slow rhythms of the office equipment; he had finally remembered.

How long has it been?

He slowly removed his blanket and gazed at the bandage covering his latest mistake. It had not hurt as much as it had before. He swiftly realized a tube connected to his wrist.

The memory had felt so real that Samual had to really think about his predicament.

I was shot and brought to the hospital; Freight Train is dead. That was so many years ago.

He felt overwhelmed and confused.

"Good morning." A pleasant voice emerged from the curtains. A heavy-set, light-skinned woman stepped through the curtains. Her red curly hair ran down her back and reflected the sun from the window behind him. It made her seem angelic. "You've been having nightmares, huh?"

"I don't particularly like hospitals," he replied.

"Good news then," she uttered. "It looks like you may be out of here sooner than you think!"

She reached underneath his bed and grabbed a small basin, and went to the sink in the corner of the room to fill it up. Samual was in a daze and couldn't be certain if he heard her correctly.

"You are letting me go?"

"Well, yes," she responded. "Personally, if it were up to me, I'd keep you a little while longer, but doctor's orders and all."

"How long have I been here?" he asked, almost afraid to hear the answer.

"A little over a week now."

A week!

He couldn't even imagine not being out on the street for that long. The things that could've happened while he was lying in a hospital!

"Thank you, but I need to go now."

"No, no dear. Not yet." Samual had tried to get up, but the kind nurse gently laid him back down on the bed. "Just rest for now and we'll let you go in the morning."

The morning felt like an eternity away, but there was nothing he could do in the meantime. He figured he may as well cooperate.

"Excuse me, nurse," Samual had to ask.

"What is it, dear?"

"Have I had any visitors at all?"

"There was someone. But unless they were family, we couldn't let them in to see you."

"A girl!?" Samual's heart almost stopped.

"Oh no, I'm sorry, dear. You were expecting a girlfriend?" She giggled, and Sam flushed. She must've known he was here; it was all over the news. When the newscaster reported on him, she would've seen it, right? "You rest up now, sweetheart. The doctor will be here to give you one last look, and we'll leave you for the night and discharge you in the morning. OK?"

Samual nodded and turned away to face the window. Just as the nurse said, the doctor came in and gave him his clean bill of health and a lecture on staying out of trouble. Sam's mind fled elsewhere.

Why didn't she come to see me?

That night was restless. Sam's body refused to sleep in fear of reliving the same dream from the previous night. The sight of the warehouse in his mind haunted him. But while he was awake, all he could think about was seeing Samantha.

He gazed out at the city through his window, drifting into sleep for several minutes at a time until morning came. The process was lengthy, and Sam was in no mood; his body simply swayed from signature to consultation until he found himself on the steps of the hospital.

What now?

He froze for moments until hurried aside by a distressed middle-aged man. He was muttering something about being a father. Sam stood there, confused. His feet began to move on instinct.

The city was alive. The same hustle and bustle he was used to. He had to brush off a couple of corner store clerks and alleyway salesmen trying to coerce him into whatever piece of junk they were selling today. Kids were running and screaming while their parents relaxed and enjoyed the cloudless morning. It was as if nothing had changed. He had spent the majority of his energy wondering what was happening without him, and it turns out, it was absolutely nothing.

"Hey, it's you!"

Sam turned to see a man standing with a guitar strapped to his back.

"They finally let you out."

Anton?

"They wouldn't tell me if you were OK. What are the odds of running into you here?" Anton clutched his guitar strap and smiled softly at Sam.

"Do I know you?" Sam tried to play stupid.

"Well, not really, but I saw you bleeding out a week ago

and got you to the hospital. I'm glad you're OK!" Anton just stood there. His intentions were honest, but he looked as if he didn't know what to do now that Sam was there.

"So." They both stood there awkwardly. "I guess I owe you my life?"

"Hey, Stormboy isn't always going to be around to save the day. We all got to do our part." Anton smiled lightly. "He saved my life once, you know."

"Is that right?" Sam responded.

"Yeah. It was something else. Probably should've died that night. But he had my back. The least I could do is try and do the same for someone else."

"Well, thank you. I don't know how to repay you."

"No, please, you don't have to do anything. Stormboy wouldn't ask anything in return."

Sam laughed and nodded.

"I mean, if you have to do something, you can come watch me perform. A friend and I play downtown most nights. You should come by!"

"I think I could do that." Sam and Anton shook hands and parted ways.

Sam turned the corner to his street and noticed Marlene and Vanessa, Darius's girls, laughing and playing hopscotch. They sang a song as they held each other's hands, swinging around. Marlene let go of Vanessa suddenly, and she slapped her butt on the concrete.

"Why did you do that?" Vanessa screamed. She wiped tears from her eyes through her unkempt bangs. She had so much hair it looked like a mane. Sam ran to the girl to see if she was OK.

"No, no, Sam, leave her." Darius called from above. He had been hovering over the two girls from the front porch of the apartment building on the second floor. "Leave her. She's fine, aren't you, baby?"

Vanessa got up, rubbing her butt. Marlene looked distressed, not sure whether she should apologize or continue playing.

"That's right, baby. Marlene! Be careful. That's your sister. You are supposed to take care of her!"

"Yes, Daddy," Marlene responded obediently, and the two began singing their songs again.

"Sam! Where have you been?" Sam, caught off guard, began to make his way up the stairs to join Darius. "Haven't seen you in a while partner; is everything OK?"

Do I tell him the truth? Tell him I was shot?

"Just got out of the hospital."

Halfway through a swig of beer, he jerked, almost spitting it onto Sam.

"Oh shit, are you OK?"

"Yeah, nothing serious. I'm fine." Sam instinctually rubbed his bullet wound. "Your girls are still getting into trouble I see."

"Yeah, man. My angels!" Darius looked on with pride. "Vanessa's a little firecracker, always doing things she knows she ain't supposed to, like getting swung around too FAST!"

His voice boomed to the streets below, and the girls began to slow their spinning. Darius continued.

"But she's got a good heart and is always trying to make me and her sister laugh. And Marlene, she's my rock. She's more of a parent to Vanessa than I am sometimes. She reminds me so much of her mother."

Sam lost himself in his words and couldn't help but ask.

"Why didn't you let me help Vanessa when she fell?"

"She's old enough. At some point, she has to learn that she can't always depend on others. She has to stand up, brush herself off, and do things on her own. I'm a single parent. I can't take care of them forever."

The two sat in silence, just watching the two of them. Occasionally, Darius would interject as the two girls wandered too close to the street or out of view of the balcony. Otherwise, it was just silence. At any point Sam could have gone inside, but something urged him to stay. Darius was the first to speak out.

"So, we haven't had any early morning nuisances in a while." Darius had a smooth grin on his face. Sam's face got hot.

"You really aren't going to let this go, are you?" Sam blushed a bit. "Like I said, she was just helping me out for a bit. That's it."

"Whoa, whoa, whatever you say, man," Darius laughed. "You ask her out yet?"

The thought passed through him and reminded him of the night in midtown at the City Hall.

"We did have one night," he reminisced. Sam had never opened up to anyone about Samantha like this before. Who would he open up to?

"Hang on a sec," Darius said and motioned to go inside. "Watch the girls for me?"

Sam nodded, confused. From the overhead view, Sam saw the pictures on the ground the girls had drawn. Several numbered boxes for their game with various creatures flying and dancing around them. Sam watched them play and tried to think of a time for himself when life was that simple, but before he could finish his thought, Darius returned. Two new bottles of beer in hand. He passed one to Sam.

"Talk to me, man." Darius twisted the top and took a long swig. Sam mimicked him and immediately convulsed at the bitterness of the beverage. "Not much of a drinker?"

"No, it's fine," Sam said, embarrassed.

OK, you can do this.

He took another swig, if only to prove to Darius he was some semblance of normal.

"So, what's her name?"

"Samantha."

Darius let out a deep, throated chuckle.

"Sam and Sam! Sounds like a good fit!" Samual couldn't help but laugh, too. It had felt like destiny to him, but there was that lingering doubt. "There's something wrong though, huh?"

He could sense it. Whether it was his eyes that were cast to the floor, or the tone in his voice. Regardless, it was written all over Sam.

"She's a nurse, and the whole time I was in the hospital, she didn't come see me once."

"Maybe she was busy. You can't hold that against her."

Maybe Darius was right, nursing is a serious job. Who knows, maybe she wasn't allowed to see him.

"Do you like this girl?" Darius's question came suddenly, and although the answer seemed obvious, he found it hard to say out loud.

"I don't know." The words spilled out of him.

"I'm gonna tell you a story, kid." Darius spoke in such a tone that it reminded him of Mr. Kain. He stood at attention, taking sips of his drink. "I think I was about your age when this happened to me. It was a Friday night. Me and a few of the boys were downtown. It was any other night—dancing girls, loud music, and liquor, ya know?"

Samual didn't, but he pretended for Darius's sake.

"Not sure if it was the second or third spot, but out of the corner of my eye, I see the baddest chick I have ever seen in my entire life. Slim waist, big hips, curls for days and her hazel eyes caught me through the club like she was begging me to come over!"

"So, you went and talked to her, right?"

"Hell no!" His answer surprised Sam. "I found some chick that night, and it ended up not working out in the long run."

"I'm confused."

"Well, eventually, I saw the same chick months, if not a year, later. I knew from the first time I saw her all that time ago that she was the right one, but I let it slide for the easy bait. We got together, and now I have my two beautiful baby girls."

"What happened to her?"

Darius's mood quickly soured. He brought the bottle to his lips once more before answering.

"Cancer." He let out a long sigh. "She was stolen from us, Sam."

"I'm so sorry."

"I could've had her so much earlier if only I had taken my shot. What I would give for a second longer. For my girls to have a second longer."

The two of them watched the girls play in silence.

"Sorry, I didn't mean to bring you down like that. I do enjoy talking about her. Just sometimes I get to thinking about how much I miss her. What I'm saying is, Sam, you got something you think is right. You gotta go for it! Don't waste time like I did. Or else you're going to regret every second, I promise you."

Sam finished his drink and headed inside. The place seemed abandoned. He took a moment to lay himself out on the couch. He rubbed his wound and let his mind wander.

What am I doing?

The smooth white ceiling transported him somewhere far away. Images of Samantha's face surrounded by electricity. Her smile kept him warm, but if he looked anywhere else, all he saw were corpses. People he had hurt in the past and potential scenarios he would find himself in. Despite the carnage, she continued to smile. Her constant and steady smile.

"Everything for them," he whispered to himself. "But what about me?"

Samual got to his feet, winced at the slight pain he felt in his stomach, but proceeded regardless. Darius was ushering his girls back inside. With a smile on his face, he spoke out.

"Wish him luck, girls!"

The two girls responded in unison. "Good luck, Mr. Sam!"

He barely paid any attention to them as he rushed down the stairs. Everything in his life up to this moment felt complicated and confusing, but this was simple! He didn't want to say the words, but what else could it be?

I have to see her!

Mr. Kain's words kept coming back to him like a hurricane. "Love is a distraction!" But he brushed it away. Nothing was going to stop him. Not this time. Mr. Kain had controlled his life for too long. It was time he stopped living for them and started living for himself. Stop living as Stormboy and start being Sam!

He took to a full sprint. His streets were never more pleasurable to navigate.

Everything for them!

The words shocked him again. No way was Mr. Kain going to steal this from him. Every time he thought about her, his heart fluttered. How could that possibly be a bad thing?

Everything for them. But today is mine!

Her apartment was finally in view. He was finally going to let her know everything he felt about her. There was much more commotion than he was expecting. Some large trucks were parked out front of her complex, and Samual had to maneuver himself past some large men carrying furniture. He finally made it to the front of the building, and he noticed the same guys from before hanging out on the stoop.

"Ay, it's that guy from before!" He had the same brown bag in his hands. Sam was eager to ignore him, but being clearly drunk he made it impossible.

"Where's Samantha?"

"Give her a second. She'll be out in a minute. Chick is busy today. I'm gonna miss her fine ass!"

Miss her?

Two more moving guys carrying a mattress came bursting through the door of her building, followed closely by Samantha, directing them. She wore a long white tee shirt which covered her short jean shorts. Her hair had been pulled back into a ponytail; it had been straightened since the last time he saw her, but no matter what she did, she was as stunning as always. She looked as if she was struck in the face when their eyes finally met.

"Sam." Her voice saying his name felt like pure ecstasy.

"Hey, Sam." He was confused, but overall, too emotionally overwhelmed to say anything else.

"What are you doing here?"

Samual immediately flushed. Everything from this moment before was pure emotion. He had no idea what to say or how he was going to say it.

"I came to see you. I probably should've brought you something." He patted his pockets as if expecting something to be there for her. His body was fidgeting, occasionally flinching from the pain of his wound.

"Is everything OK?" The uniformed men beckoned her attention, but she quickly shooed them away to step closer to Sam.

"I just haven't seen you in a while. I was in the hospital and ..."

"You what?" She immediately cut him off.

"Yeah, injured on a job." He scratched his head, which made him wince yet again. "I guess you were right after all."

"What happened? Where were you hurt? How long were you out for? You idiot! How could you let that happen?" Her questions came before he could answer any of the previous ones. There was a time where this would have caught Samual off guard, but expecting the unexpected was commonplace with her. That thought put a smile on his face. "Why are you smiling?"

"I'm just really glad to see you." The men squeezed past the two carrying large boxes.

I really should have gotten her something.

Samantha sighed.

"I'm just glad you're OK." Samantha placed a hand on his cheek, but before he could grab it, she pulled away.

"I was expecting to see you at the hospital, but you never came."

"The last couple of days have been a bit crazy."

"Ma'am where would you like this?" the men interrupted, carrying a couch, clearly struggling.

"That goes on the truck with you. Thanks."

"Am I interrupting something?" Samual was slowly trying to piece together the scene. He had been on countless stake-outs, watching thieves make their way with furniture in the same way, but this mundane situation threw him.

"Sam, we need to talk." Samantha took his hand and guided him away from prying eyes. He assumed she'd take him to her apartment, but instead, they hid on the side of the building for some semblance of privacy.

Sam had never felt so happy, yet so out of place in his life. Samantha was pacing before him. He waited for her to stop and formulate her words, but she just kept pacing.

"Did I do something wrong? I thought you would be happy to see me," Sam pondered. Samantha finally turned to him.

"Sam. My dad is dead." She was clearly distressed; Sam went to approach her, but she pulled away.

"I'm so sorry. Is there anything I can do?"

"No, it's fine. Thank you, but . . ."

"Is there something you want to tell me?" he said, still confused. Samantha crossed her arms before speaking again.

"I'm going to miss you, Sam."

"What are you talking about?"

What is she talking about?

"My mom needs me. I'm going to go take care of her. So, I'm leaving."

His vision went dark. It was the hardest punch he had ever received in his life.

"So, when will you be back?" he asked the question, but he had a feeling he already knew the answer.

"No Sam, I don't think you understand." This felt famil-iar. It was Mr. Kain talking down to him again. It was the Williames telling him they didn't want him anymore. It made him feel like a boy. "I don't think I am coming back."

Sam turned his head to the sky in a way to stop the tears from falling. He forced a smile.

"I'm sorry. I was hoping to leave before I got a chance to see you again. I know it sounds awful, and I'm sorry. This is best for both of us, I think. I know it may not seem like it now, but it is."

"I just thought that . . . I mean I got shot and . . ."

"Wait—you got shot?" She immediately began inspecting his body despite him trying to push her away. "Where? How bad?"

"It doesn't matter."

"It doesn't matter?"

"No! It doesn't!" He was sure the entire complex heard his outburst, but he didn't care anymore. "When I was laying in the hospital, I just kept thinking where you were. Will I see you again? How can you say that this is best for us? How do you know what's best for me?"

"Sam."

"No! This whole time you've been asking me what I want and what I want to do. What I want is you! What I want to do is be with you!"

He hadn't realized it until that moment. As the tears streamed down his face, his talent was flaring. Once his screaming had stopped, he could hear the cracking of lightning flowing around him. Samantha didn't flinch. She wasn't afraid of him. She closed in and cupped his chin, wiping away a tear with her thumb. Her hair began to levitate as the static transferred between them.

"That isn't up to just you." Her hand felt warm. He wanted to live in her cupped hands forever. "You are a really good person, Sam."

"You're all I want." He grabbed her hand and tried to ease her closer to him.

"Sam, no." She pulled away. "You may not believe it right now, but I want what's best for you. But what's best for you isn't me."

"Then what is best for me?"

Samantha smiled.

"Haven't you been paying attention? That's something you have to decide for yourself." Samantha broke away. "I'm sorry, but I have to go."

She began to make her way around the building.

"Sam," she uttered before rounding the corner of her complex, "I will miss you."

She brushed down her static hair and disappeared around the corner. To Samual, the world seemed the same yet completely different, all at the same time. His mind kept on searching for some sort of guidance, some sort of knowledge from the past he could apply to make himself feel less like himself at this moment. But for the first time ever, his mind was silent.

He wanted to go back to the cemetery to see Freight Train, but how could he face him like this?

Westside may as well have been a ghost town. The hustle and bustle of the city was mute to him. Sam couldn't help but keep his eyes glued to the floor and his legs made their way back to his house on pure instinct. He had just meandered through the streets for hours, trying to shake this pit in his stomach, but nothing was working. The sun began to go down, and he finally managed to make it back home. Luckily for him, Darius and his girls were already asleep at this point in the night, so he managed to make it inside uninterrupted. His house was a disaster, as per usual, but somehow it felt worse. His mind returned to that first day. The arguing neighbors, the frustration when he stopped her from cleaning, the glow of when she saw him as more than just Stormboy for the first time. His powers exploded out of him, eager to cause as much damage as possible, and Sam didn't care if it did. Lightning

126

scorched holes in his roof, floor, and furniture. It was every-thing Mr. Kain had spoken against, and he knew it, but his powers wanted out, and Sam needed the release. The untapped frustration took its toll until his home was left a wreck

CHAPTER 12

TWO YEARS AGO

It was a surprisingly silent night at this end of Westside. The lights lit the empty streets, and Stormboy felt alone for the first time in a long time. Westside General was one of the biggest buildings in the entire city, and it felt intimidating to Stormboy, especially since he knew the person he was going to see.

Was I supposed to come in costume?

He never had to question these kinds of things before now. Freight Train had always had his back. He had had an answer for everything. But now . . .

He entered the intimidating structure, and despite his unusual superhero attire, he remained surprisingly unnoticed.

"Hi, I'm here to see Freight Train . . ." The large woman behind the desk glanced up at him.

"Freight Train? Oh, honey, you mean Edward Kain? I'm so sorry, dear."

Stormboy remained silent. The woman gestured down the hall toward a room. Stormboy had half expected the hall to be flooded with reporters and fans trying to get a look at the one and only Freight Train, but his room was just like any other. Plain white tile, curtain drawn so he was not able to see the bed next to him, and a plain twin-sized bed his massive frame barely fit in. The room was so white it looked sterile. Freight Train lay in his bed, staring motionless at the ceiling. If he didn't know any better, he would have thought they sat a mannequin up in the bed to keep his identity and location a secret.

"Freight Train?" Sam said quietly. Mr. Kain remained as he was, a world away. Stormboy approached the bed. It wasn't until he was close enough to his side that he finally acknowledged him.

"Sammy." He exhaled his words weakly.

"How are you feeling, Freight Train?" Sam replied, and Mr. Kain scoffed.

"No Freight Train. And take off that mask."

The words surprised Stormboy. He had always told him to keep the disguise up in the eyes of the public. "Take it off!"

His voice boomed through the tiny room, and Stormboy quickly obeyed. He was now Sam. Plain, ordinary Sam.

"Sammy, look at me. What was it all for?"

Sam stared silently. Was he supposed to speak? Did he really want an answer?

"All the years I spent fighting and protecting these people, and this is what I get. A blank room to die alone in."

Sam's heart stopped.

Die?

Sam knew that the tumor they had found in his brain was serious, but they were supposed to fix him! They probably would have never even seen it if it wasn't for that warehouse fight they had got into.

"Somehow, I expected more out of all this," Mr. Kain continued. "What's the sense in it all if this is where you end up?"

"Well, you always told me that the job itself was reward enough," Sam said nervously; he was still reeling from the previous statement. Mr. Kain let out a weak laugh.

"Yeah. Another one of my goddamn slogans." Mr. Kain

finally turned to Sam. "What is the number one rule?"

"Everything for them."

"Everything for them! Don't ever forget that."

A nurse knocked on the door.

"Mr. Kain, you have another visitor." Mr. Kain's demeanor shifted drastically. Suddenly, he was trying to sit up straight, and Sam could've sworn some color returned to his face. His nurse ushered in a man in his late forties, tall, dark-skinned, and dressed in a fine suit, who stopped only to remove his sunglasses.

"Edward," he said solemnly. Mr. Kain slumped back down again, clearly disappointed.

"Mayor Warren." Mr. Kain attempted to sit up, but it sapped all the energy out of him. Everything came out raspy like his voice had given up on him.

"How are you feeling, old friend?" the mayor asked.

Samual had met the man a few times, for him to call himself a friend to Mr. Kain was being generous. Samual immediately checked behind him to make sure no paparazzi were following him, as they tended to when he made visits to the illustrious Freight Train.

"Like shit." Mr. Kain's response was direct; he refused to make eye contact.

"If there is anything we can do to make your stay more comfortable. Hang on." The mayor hollered at a nurse for more pillows and blankets, anything they could find. That was his style. He threw his money and influence around until whoever he was trying to impress liked him. Sam hated him, but he was a necessary evil. Or at least Mr. Kain had always said he was.

"Now is not the time, Gabe." Again, he pushed the words out, struggling. The mayor crept toward the bedside. He looked lost, like there was something he should be doing but didn't quite know what that was. An awkward hush came over the room.

130

Should I say something?

The three of them remained silent, Mr. Kain avoiding the mayor's gaze.

"Is there something you wanted, Mr. Mayor?" Every time he spoke, he held back another cough or moan. It was clearly a struggle for him, but even toward the end, he refused to show weakness.

"I just came to pay my respects. The city owes you two so much."

"Thank you," Mr. Kain replied. He wanted to cut him off quickly. "I think I'd like to be alone with my ward now. If you don't mind."

"Of course." He seemed relieved to be dismissed. If he had to stay any longer, Sam thought the mayor's head would've exploded. Sam escorted him out of the room. When Sam turned to face Freight Train again, his head was buried in his hands.

Is he crying?

"Freight Train?" He approached cautiously. Before he could react, Mr. Kain reached out and grabbed his sleeve and pulled him so close their noses almost touched.

"Promise me!"

It had been the first time he had ever seen tears on his face. It was somehow odd and terrifying. The mentor he had looked up to all these years now seemed as fragile as everyone else. He was human. Sam, so overcome with emotion, began to cry, too.

"Promise me, Stormboy! You will not give up the fight! Let nothing deter you. Everything for them! You must cast aside everything else!" Samual nodded his head vigorously. He didn't mean to show fear, but Mr. Kain's outburst made him tremble.

"Yes, sir." Sam managed to squeeze out a reply.

"Connection is cancer!"

"Connection is cancer." Sam parroted his words.

"No attachments, no distractions! Say it!"

"No distractions."

"What else?"

"No attachments."

"Why?"

"Because everything for them!" Sam hadn't realized he was trying to pull away from him until Mr. Kain released his grip, and Sam toppled backwards onto the floor.

"You have to be better than me, Samual. Take what I've taught you and learn from it." He turned to Sam. "You are my legacy. Promise me."

He acknowledged, as all good wards did. As all good sons should.

Something inside of him knew, as he walked out of that room, that this was the last time he would ever see Freight Train. At his mentor's request, Sam closed the door behind him. He was the hero of Westside now. The fluorescent lighting in the hospital's hall did nothing to brighten anything at all. His heart felt dark and heavy. Samual put on his mask. Being Stormboy never felt more important than it had in this moment. Thankfully, the mask covered his tears. He straightened himself up and prepared to face the world alone. The hall was sterile white as he remembered, except for one major difference. There had been a woman. Her body pressed against the wall; she had a fancy red dress that cut up the side. She had stuck out from the rest. She held a handkerchief to her face to catch the tears streaming from her face; she looked troubled. Stormboy met her eyes for a moment. She had a flash of familiarity toward him.

"You're him," she said softly. Sam stared at her; she was grasping for words that wouldn't come.

No attachments. No distractions. Everything for them.

Sam turned and walked away from her. She became sterile, like everything else.

CHAPTER 13

MOVING FORWARD

How many days has it been?

Clothes and takeout food containers were thrown about his home, and he was oblivious to it all. Sam would tune into the news and hear of rampant crime in the absence of "super-powered assistance." Even after all this time, they couldn't say his name and put a positive spin on it. It didn't matter. Besides, how could they possibly understand? Samantha was gone, and he was a shell. He had gone back a week later just to be sure. It was late. He knocked before electrifying the lock off the door. But it was true. Completely barren—only noise coming from the muted conversations of her old neighbors. Sam sat in the middle of her living room that entire night, remembering their final moments together.

A knock came at his door.

"Sam, are you there?" The voice was undeniably Darius's. "Sam, you need to open up now, man!"

For what? Why can't he just leave me alone?

Darius was relentless. He spent fifteen minutes in his pursuit until Sam eventually caved in. The chain on his door held tight as he peaked through. Darius was alone, his girls nowhere in sight. Sam found that particularly odd, but didn't question it.

"Sam, where have you been? No one has seen you go in or out in weeks!"

"I've been here. What's the problem?"

"The problem? You don't see a problem?" Darius said.

"Leave me alone." Sam attempted to close the door on him, but Darius wedged a foot to prevent him.

"No way, son. You are going to open this door, and we are going to talk about whatever the hell is going on with you right now."

Sam's body acted on its own. Before he knew it, he was undoing the latch, and Darius stood face to face with him.

"All right, talk," Darius said forcefully.

"Ain't nothing to say." Sam made his way to his kitchen and poured himself a glass of wine.

"This isn't like you. Mrs. Ramirez is starting to worry, too."

"Why do you care? Why do any of you care?"

"I wouldn't be here right now if I didn't care, Sammy."

"Don't call me that." His sudden reaction caused him to spill the wine from his glass; he held it so tight he was afraid he might crush it in his palm. Darius approached slowly, took the glass out of his hand, and placed his hand on his shoulder.

"What happened?"

"She's gone." His voice cracked. "She just left. If you didn't tell me to go after her, I might have . . ." The thought that came hurt more than he expected.

I might have never seen her again.

Darius let out a sigh.

"Sam, I'm sorry."

He wiped his face, embarrassed.

"It doesn't matter. It was stupid to begin with. Mr. Kain always taught me, no distractions."

"Of course it matters! How you feel about something always matters. Allow yourself to grieve, but this here has to stop." Darius gestured to his entire place. The filth and decay his home had undergone was greater than it ever had been. Pieces of the wallpaper were scorched from his power being let loose. A table had toppled over that he never bothered to fix, and everything that could possibly be on the floor was there. Mail from weeks ago, half-full containers, and, of course, the wine.

"You are allowed to feel and be sad, but this isn't helping anybody."

"Then what am I supposed to do?" Sam bellowed. Darius guided Sam to his couch. He sighed heavily before speaking.

"The day my wife died was the worst day of my life. The doctor had confirmed for some time that the day was coming, but how do you ever prepare for something like that? She was doing all she could to stay with us so her family could come and say their last goodbyes, but in all honesty, I think she was doing it to keep me from falling apart. It was a Wednesday. I remember it being hot as hell, and I was walking home. Had to sell the car to pay for her treatments. I had just picked up the girls from school when we got the call that she was fading and didn't have much time. I carried both Marlene and Vanessa and started running. I knew how far we were; it was at least a half an hour on foot, and there was no way I was waiting on a damn bus. So I kept running, knowing full well what I was running into. My girls were confused. Marlene may have understood, but Vanessa just wanted to go home and play. Both were crying and carrying on, but all that mattered was getting to her. We finally arrived, but it was too late. She was gone. The glow faded from her skin, and no matter how much I hugged her, she wouldn't move. My lady was gone."

"What did you do?" Sam asked.

"I explained to the girls that they would never see their mother again, and the three of us went home."

Sam was taken aback.

"Your wife just died! How could you possibly just go home?"

"Marlene and Vanessa hadn't eaten yet. I couldn't afford to take a day off from work, especially since I had a funeral to pay for now."

"But she was the love of your life. You told me she was everything to you."

"She was, Sammy, and don't you ever think otherwise." His voice rose suddenly. "But life went on. There were people who needed me. I grieved for a long time, but I also knew I had to keep going, for my girls' sake."

Sam's chest felt heavy, but it alleviated after Darius slapped him hard on the back.

"I'm not going to tell you how to grieve. But you got to keep moving." Sam kept his gaze low in his drink. With another pat on the shoulder, Darius stood to leave. "This city still needs its hero."

Sam looked up at him suddenly.

"How did you . . .?" Sam questioned.

"Kid, I've always known." Darius gave him a quick wink before leaving him alone.

For some reason, it hadn't come as much of a surprise to Sam. He smiled softly and reflected on his words. It was such a simple concept. Moving forward. He retreated to his wine bottle but hesitated. He spent so much time feeling sorry for himself he hadn't thought about what would come next.

Everything for them.

What do you want?

Move forward.

Everything snapped into place. Sam poured the wine down the drain and ran to get dressed. He felt a slight chill as he pulled his uniform over his head and affixed his mask to his face. Electricity radiated off him. Sam snuck out of the back porch into the city.

The streets felt like his again. He climbed the sides of the apartment structures effortlessly. He sprang from rooftop to rooftop; the wind kissing his face as a reminder of his purest self. Streams of lightning trailed him as he leapt off buildings, landing on to a fence before flipping off into a full sprint. Despite how long he had been away, the streets accepted him once more.

Then he arrived. The cemetery sign loomed ominously. Once this place had scared him, a place he felt like he should avoid. Not today, though. He approached the steps to the large grey mausoleum; the large stone pillars were as daunting as ever.

"Back again, I see." Ron must have noticed him walking in. He held up the key to the place, correctly assuming why he'd been there. Sam entered the tomb. The door groaned heavily as it revealed the same large chamber he'd grown accustomed to.

Freight Train's statue stood as imposing as ever. He had never been here while the sun was up. With the light of the afternoon sun, Sam noticed some details of the statue he hadn't before. Rust began to settle on his shiny golden finish. What was once a brilliant tribute to Westside's greatest hero was a dull imitation of its former self. The large smile on his face that had been a vision of inspiration was now eroded and smoothed over. He looked emotionless and hard.

"Hey, Mr. Kain." His hushed tones still echoed throughout the chamber. "I know it's been a while, but I'm here."

The statue stared back in silence.

"You've given me so much. When no one wanted to take me in, you gave me a home. While others saw my abilities as a burden, you saw them as gifts. You raised me to be a hero, and I can't ever repay you enough for that. With everything you gave me, I was afraid to ask for anything more."

Sam straightened himself and moved to the statue's feet.

"I've spent my entire life trying to please everyone else in this city. I felt it was the only way to honor your memory. To be your perfect little soldier. I sacrificed everything else. But I deserve more than that. Am I not allowed to live outside of all this? Outside of Stormboy? You made your choices, and in the end you died alone. For what?"

Sam stared at the statue, expecting a response for some reason. Maybe he wanted validation for his ranting.

"I can't be you. I never could have been. The problem is, I never should have tried. You're gone now. There will never be another Edward Kain, and no matter how much they cry and complain about me and the way I do things, I'm making a difference and I'm doing it my way. I wanted to be the next Freight Train, but I couldn't. But Sam . . . I can be him."

He placed his hand on the foot of the statue, then turned and left.

Ron was sitting right outside, waiting for him.

"So, you gonna be back, boy?"

"Maybe," Sam smiled. "But not for a while."

CHAPTER 14

FOR SAM

"Would you relax?" Tony said to Vincent. It was the dead of night, and they were waiting under the only working streetlamp on Forty-Third, as directed by their buyer. It was an unusual situation, but the score on this one deal would set them up for a while.

"I don't like this, Tony!" Vincent was a young kid fresh out of high school and wasn't used to a drug deal of this caliber. He fidgeted with the gun in his pocket and paced rapidly, taking extra care not to stray from the lamp light like a frightened child who had been ordered to stay put by his mother. Tony rolled his eyes and went back to look out for the van.

"They're taking a while. They said they'd be here at two," Vincent said nervously. Tony checked his watch. The buyer was ten minutes late. If it hadn't been for the million-dollar payout he was promised, Tony would have been gone. You should never have to wait around for stuff like this. That's how the idiots get caught.

"We'll give 'em ten more minutes," Tony replied.

"This is stupid. I'm sure we can find another buyer. Let's just go!" The kid was right, but a million dollars was a million dollars.

"What are you so worried about? Not like we got the Storm kid on our back." It had been six weeks since anyone saw Stormboy. There were some gangs that were still wary, but now was the best time for a deal like this. It had been strange, though. All the years he had been worried about Stormboy. It wasn't like him to be gone for so long. But when Tony saw an opportunity, he took it.

Five more minutes passed, and Vincent was getting even more restless. Tony was ready to put a bullet in him himself if it meant shutting him up. At least then he could keep all the money for himself!

Just then, Tony realized something. He perked his ear up at a noise in the distance.

"Shut up!" Tony insisted. Vincent immediately drew his gun. The noise was getting closer, he was sure of it. Gunfire! Tony followed Vincent and drew his gun, aiming it down the street where the noise was coming from. Headlights appeared as a car came flying around the corner a few blocks down. It was going fast! It swerved back and forth, ramming into parked cars on either side of the road. Vincent couldn't stop himself from shooting wildly at the out-of-control vehicle.

"What are you doing?" Tony screamed, forcing Vincent to lower his gun. The car was approaching rapidly. Tony noticed out of the front seat, a streak of electrical energy shot out the window and a figure leapt out as the car swerved one more time. It was now heading straight for them.

"Get down!" Tony yelled as he grabbed Vincent and dove out of the way of the car, which crashed straight into the light post behind them. The streetlight shattered, leaving the whole street lit by the moonlight alone. Tony pulled Vincent to his feet. "Run, kid!" And the two took off down an alley. Vincent stole a moment to look back and saw a dark figure inspect the car for survivors before fixating his gaze down the alley at them.

"It's him!" Vincent said. He raised his pistol and fired two shots. The figure ducked and dodged out of the way.

"You idiot. Just run!" Tony grabbed Vincent's arm and continued running. The two couldn't be certain if they were being followed, but they knew if they stopped it would be over. Then it hit Tony.

"Split up!" he said.

"What?" Vincent replied.

"He won't catch us if we split up!" Tony and Vincent stopped for a moment. Tony knew that wasn't entirely true. The truth was, he probably would catch at least one of them. This gave him the best chance of getting away himself. "You head that way, and we'll meet up at the usual spot."

"I don't know if that's such a good idea," Vincent said.

"Go!" Tony shoved Vincent in the opposite direction and took off. Vincent didn't like it, but what else was he going to do? Tony vanished around a corner, and Vincent was alone. With one hand firmly on his pistol in his pocket, he took off. That thing was chasing them—could it really have been Stormboy? He seemed different from the stories he heard somehow. Whatever it was seemed more serious, more intense. Those eyes he saw before he shot at him, they almost seemed dangerous, not like the hero of Westside, but a wild force of nature. A shadow passed through the alley in front of Vincent, and he immediately pulled out his weapon again. The echoes of far-off sirens filled the alley.

"I knew this was a bad idea," he whispered. A glass tipped over, clanging against the floor, which caused Vincent to jump and fire his weapon prematurely. "Just show yourself already!"

A shadow revealed itself from the rooftops just above him. It leapt from the rooftop down the fire escape of the neighboring apartment buildings. Vincent fired wildly off into the air, eventually tripping and stumbling backwards. The shadow stood over him. They both locked their eyes. Vincent couldn't believe what he saw. It was him! Lightning streamed off his back and into his palm, illuminating them both in the darkness of the alley. Vincent had always heard Stormboy wore a hood and some dumb spray-painted T-shirt, but this guy was different. He wore a dark blue overcoat with a solid black shirt underneath. On his face, a black cloth covered the lower half of his face and a mask that made his eyes glow an eerie glossy white. He always thought he was just some sort of hoodlum like him, but this man looked unearthly. Like a phantom. The masked man knelt next to him.

"You shot at me," the man said in a low tone. Vincent threw the gun away and put his hands above his head.

The police had finally arrived at the scene and saw two men were already tied up and pouting on the side of the street with a strange cloaked figure looming over them. The police drew their weapons and aimed at the unfamiliar man.

"Hands up. Now!"

"These two were a part of a drug deal going down. All the goods are in that briefcase there." The man gestured to a case leaning against one of the tied-up men. "The ones they were selling to are off Forty-Third, the car is wrecked, and the three inside are incapacitated."

The cops were clearly caught off guard. The man put forth a powerful yet familiar energy. The officer couldn't quite place it. An officer went over to retrieve the case and verify its contents, while a second radioed to check for the car on Forty-Third.

"If you have it under control here, the night is young, and I'm needed elsewhere," the man said.

"Is that you, Stormboy?" the cop wondered, lowering his weapon.

The man smiled. "No, not Stormboy. Not anymore."

"Well, who do we have to thank for this?"

"Just call me Sam."

ABOUT ATMOSPHERE PRESS

Founded in 2015, Atmosphere Press was built on the principles of Honesty, Transparency, Professionalism, Kindness, and Making Your Book Awesome. As an ethical and author-friendly hybrid press, we stay true to that founding mission today.

If you're a reader, enter our giveaway for a free book here:

SCAN TO ENTER
BOOK GIVEAWAY

If you're a writer, submit your manuscript for consideration here:

SCAN TO SUBMIT
MANUSCRIPT

And always feel free to visit Atmosphere Press and our authors online at atmospherepress.com. See you there soon!

ABOUT THE AUTHOR

Starting with a dream to make films, author Craig Robinson started as a script writer, writing short films and editing small works such as screenplays and novels for other aspiring writers. Jealous of his clients creating stories, Craig is ready to venture and amaze you with his rich character studies in the Fantasy genre. Born in New York and raised in South Florida, he brings a unique flavor to his work that we know you will find endlessly entertaining.

)